G000089423

The Fun of Motivation:

Crossing the Threshold Concepts

By Mary Francis

Association of College and Research Libraries
A division of the American Library Association
Chicago, Illinois 2017

The paper used in this publication meets the minimum requirements of American National Standard for Information Sciences–Permanence of Paper for Printed Library Materials, ANSI Z39.48-1992. ∞

Cataloging-in-Publication data is on file with the Library of Congress.

Printed in the United States of America.

21 20 19 18 17 5 4 3 2 1

Contents

Acknowledgements

Part I is an expansion of the article "Using Fun to Teach Rigorous Content," first published in *Communications in Information Literacy* in 2012.

I would like to dedicate this book to Christopher who always pushes me to excel. And to Henry and Hazel, may you be filled with a lifelong desire for new information and the skills to think about it critically.

Introduction

The inspiration for this book came from two different but eventually over-lapping areas. The first was the relationship of fun to education. As an instruction librarian, I am always learning and exploring new ways to improve the instruction I offer. To that end, I attended Immersion Teacher Track, I joined the ACRL Instruction Section, I followed blogs, I read the professional literature, I watched webinars, I took part in ACRL's Assessment in Action program, I earned a second master's degree in technology for education and training, and I paid attention to any mention of teaching in my daily life. From all these experiences, I learned and continue to learn much that I apply when I plan and offer instruction sessions.

Periodically within these experiences, I would hear the word *fun*. It was not stressed heavily, but it was a regular occurrence. I began to wonder about the place of fun within education. For me, learning has always been fun. That is part of the appeal of the library and reference and instruction. I am always able to learn something new as I assist patrons and students with their varied research needs. This is the *Trivial Pursuit* aspect of my personality, where every new tidbit of learning is interesting. However, I also know that many people do not share this innate appreciation for learning. So I began to question what it meant to refer to education and fun together. As I tried to think through this connection, I started writing notes from my stream of consciousness. This is one from my files.

> Several of the articles refer to the use of games and humor as a way to make the library and librarians "approachable and fun." It is very important for librarians to be approachable. We answer questions. If we cannot be approached to hear the question, we will not be of use. But fun? Is it important for librarians to be fun? Often the biggest compliment a student can give to their friends about a class is that the teacher is fun. Are fun classes good classes? Learning

1

or perhaps growth as a learner is the most important part of an instructional session. Where is the place of fun within this goal? Are you more likely to pay attention and develop if you are having fun? Does having a "fun" class lower your status as a serious professional? What is the place of fun in a classroom? What is the place of humor? Are fun and humor interchangeable? Can everyone be fun? Are there skills and techniques that can be applied to increase one's "funness"? What is fun? What characteristics make a class fun? Is there a line between being a teacher and being fun? Is fun the same as interesting? If someone is fun, do they lose respect? Of students? Of peers? Is fun the same for everyone? What classes did you learn the most in? What classes did you have the most fun in? Were they the same? Did fun classes allow for more time to grow as an individual, interact with others, open up? Think of a time you had fun learning something. What did you learn? Why was it fun? What is the place of fun in learning?

As can be seen, there were several questions relating to whether fun really is something appropriate to integrate into the classroom. But also of note were the questions inquiring as to what exactly is fun. Without having a clear definition and understanding of what is meant by fun, it is not possible to analyze its use within the classroom.

The second area that inspired this book was a faculty professional development session held on my campus. In part, the presenter discussed Raymond Wlodkowski's book *Enhancing Adult Motivation to Learn: A Guide to Improving Instruction and Increasing Learner Achievement.*[1] The part that really caught my attention was the preventer's comment that when we learn something, we reach a learning edge where learning becomes uncomfortable because it is difficult or beyond our understanding. Since we do not like the uncomfortable feeling of moving beyond our current knowledge, some individuals will simply fall back on what they already know. This is a critical point, because if you do not move beyond the edge you are stuck with limited knowledge. If you stay on the edge, you start to associate learning with a negative feeling, which can result in a dislike for the whole process of learning. So to move beyond this edge, motivation comes into play to help the individual get beyond the unknown and back into a comfortable position of understanding. This continual cycle of frustration and resolution develops an ever-increasing string of understanding and ability as we develop deeper learning.

The concept of motivating students to get past this point of learning where they are stuck on a topic stayed with me until it finally connected with that train of thought regarding fun. Could fun be used as a motivating technique to help students get past the learning edge? I started to see how fun could have a place within the classroom if it was used with consideration in order to meet an established goal. This allowed me to focus my approach toward fun and create a list of fun instructional techniques that met an established definition.

One final event that confirmed my desire to explore this connection in more depth was the development of the new *Framework for Information Literacy in Higher Education*. The *Framework* moved from providing a list of standards to listing out threshold concepts, "ideas in any discipline that are passageways or portals to enlarged understanding or ways of thinking and practicing within that discipline."[2] Threshold concepts are transformative, irreversible, integrative, bounded, and potentially troublesome.

Due to their very nature, threshold concepts are ideas found on the learning edge that can create discomfort as students learn. The learning and understanding of these threshold concepts need to be facilitated with deliberation by those librarians integrating them into their instruction sessions. Students must be motivated to learn these concepts that help them master skills. I hope that in discussing the use of fun as a motivating technique to help students learn information literacy concepts, this book will help librarians approach their instruction with deliberation and perhaps a fresh light.

This book is organized into two parts. Within part I, the first chapter looks at **motivation**. While there are a wide number of motivational theories, specific attention is given to the Self-Determination Theory of intrinsic and extrinsic motivation, as it is one of the most highly cited and promoted theories on motivation within education. This chapter also provides summaries of models for the application of motivational theories within the classroom. It includes lists of motivating factors and ways to promote motivation. The chapter ends with a discussion of specific issues related to motivating students within information literacy instruction.

Chapter 2 discusses **fun** in relation to education. After defining fun, it provides information on the connection between fun and education. After looking at instructional techniques, the chapter ends with details on the three different instructional techniques that will be discussed within the book and how each of these techniques meets the definition of fun. The three instructional techniques are **humor**, **games**, and **group work**.

Chapters 3 through 5 each focus on one of the three **instructional techniques** in more depth to examine its benefits and to provide short literature reviews related to its use in education. Considerations of their use in the classroom and within a library instruction session are also provided. The chapters end by connecting the ways in which the instructional techniques can address the factors that promote intrinsic motivation as laid out in chapter 2.

Part II offers the application of the theory set up in part I. It is composed of six chapters, each addressing one of the **threshold concepts** provided in the *Framework for Information Literacy for Higher Education*. Each chapter contains three lesson plans addressing the threshold concept, one for each of the three fun instructional techniques. Each lesson plan begins with the learning objective. It then lists the procedure, which includes the audience, supplies, and time needed for the lesson. Assessment opportunities are provided, with formative assessment strategies as well as summative assessments, including sample rubrics to apply to a range of student work. Each lesson plan ends with a section on modifications and accommodations that provide discussion of the lesson if necessary and additional ideas on how to adapt the lesson for different student populations.

Just like the *Framework for Information Literacy* itself, neither these lesson plans nor this book is meant to provide a one-size-fits-all model of how to instruct students on the new threshold concepts. However, by providing theoretical context as well as examples of lesson plans, I hope to help librarians consider how they can use fun as a means to motivate students. It may also be helpful for librarians to approach the new *Framework* with a spirit of fun as we work toward the shared goal of developing information-literate students.

Notes

1. Raymond J. Wlodkowski, *Enhancing Adult Motivation to Learn* (San Francisco: Jossey-Bass, 1985).
2. Association of College and Research Libraries, *Framework for Information Literacy for Higher Education* (Chicago: Association of College and Research Libraries, 2015), 1, http://www.ala.org/acrl/standards/ilframework.

Bibliography

Association of College and Research Libraries. *Framework for Information Literacy for Higher Education*. Chicago: Association of College and Research Libraries, 2015. http://www.ala.org/acrl/standards/ilframework.

Wlodkowski, Raymond J. *Enhancing Adult Motivation to Learn: A Guide to Improving Instruction and Increasing Learner Achievement*. San Francisco: Jossey-Bass, 1985.

PART I
Background and Theory

CHAPTER 1

Motivation of Students

A wise man once observed that a great many children are like wheelbarrows: not good unless pushed. Some are like canoes: they need to be paddled. Some are like kites: if you don't keep a string on them they fly away. A few are like a good watch: open face, pure gold, quietly busy, and full of good works.[1]

Motivation

Go to any office full of cubicles or any gym full of exercise equipment, and you will be bound to see a lovely photo of a mountaintop or running legs or one of a million other inspirational things within a black outline, with the word *MOTIVATION* clearly printed beneath. Simply add a short quote, and viewers are sure to be inspired to a life full of wonder and greatness.

Unfortunately, real motivation takes more than a ten-dollar poster in a frame. Motivation is the reason we will perform a task. It is our desire to continue when exposed to difficulties and obstacles. It differs for every person and within a person from day to day. It is an important part of us, and fortunately it is something that we can develop. Motivation can be seen in all aspects of life. This book focuses specifically on the motivation to learn and looks at methods that librarians as instructors can use to help motivate the students with whom they interact.

Motivational Theories

There is no one overarching theory of motivation. Various fields and disciplines have approached motivation through different lenses. Taken in isolation, each theory makes sense and offers an explanation for why individuals are motivated to think and act. This section offers an overview of a wide range of motivation theories. Such an overview allows for a deeper appreciation of the task that instructors undertake in order to help their students develop the motivation to interact with and learn the subject content.

Maslow's Hierarchy of Needs

Maslow's Hierarchy of Needs sets forth a series of needs that must be met by an individual before that person will be able to progress to the next level. Often depicted as a pyramid, Maslow's Hierarchy posits that the motivation to complete a higher level will not be experienced until the needs of the lower levels are met. The five levels of needs, from the most basic to the highest, are physiological, safety, love/belonging, esteem, and self-actualization. Maslow's Hierarchy has been used for a number of years within a variety of disciplines and fields.[2]

Attribution Theory

According to Attribution Theory, an individual's motivation and behavior are affected by how he or she interprets past successes and failures. There are three dimensions through which the individual can interpret an event: the *locus of control*, whether the causes are internal or external; *stability*, whether the causes change over time; and *controllability*, whether the causes can be controlled by the individual. This theory suggests that past successes related to events that were in the control of the individual will be met with more motivation when similar events occur in the future.[3]

Equity Theory

The Equity Theory has a grounding in workplace motivation. It holds that when an individual feels that there is a balance between the inputs that they apply to a situation and the resulting outputs, they will be more motivated. If they feel that their inputs are not being met by significant outputs, they will be demotivated and stop working on their inputs. Example inputs include time, energy, and skill. Example outputs may include payment, recognition, or responsibility.[4]

Expectancy-Value Theory

The Expectancy-Value Theory of motivation depends on two key factors: the expectancy that the individual has of success in the activity, and the value that the individual applies to the activity. There is a sliding scale of how one can be expected to perform that is affected by past experiences and self-image. This intersects with the value that one places on the task in relation to its importance, interest, or usefulness. These combine to determine the individual's motivation to complete the activity. Motivation thereby is an individual connection based on how one relates to a specific task.[5]

Achievement Motivation Theory

The Achievement Motivation Theory builds on the Expectancy-Value Theory of motivation. In addition to the two factors—the expectancy of success and the value of the activity—one must also consider the individual's need for achievement. An individual's need for achievement can be a stable component of his or her personality, and the strength of that need will influence the level of motivation and effort that individual will apply to a given situation. Those with high need for achievement will work through more difficulties and exert more effort in order to complete an activity. They also often view achievement as a success for its own sake.[6]

Self-Efficacy Theory

The Self-Efficacy Theory identifies a simple correlation between an individual's self-efficacy and his or her motivation to work on a task until completion. The greater the self-efficacy, the more motivated the individual will be. Self-efficacy is the "conviction that one can successfully execute the behavior required to produce the outcomes."[7] Self-efficacy can be developed in students by providing them with meaningful and achievable activities that they can build upon.

Self-Worth Theory

The Self-Worth Theory focuses on an individual's sense of personal value and worth. Within this theory, individuals are motivated to perform activities that will increase their sense of self-worth. They also perform a variety of behaviors in situations where that worth is threatened. Due to the vital significance that an individual will put on self-worth, this can have a major impact on the motivation shown toward different activities.[8]

Goal Setting Theory

Goal Setting Theory is based on the idea that for people to act, they must have established a goal or end result, which supplies purpose for the action. Goals will differ in their difficulty, specificity, and commitment. McCombs and Pope developed a system to aid instructors as they develop goals for students: A—Achievable (goal is appropriate for learners), B—Believable (learners think they can do it), C—Conceivable (it is clear and measurable), and D—Desirable (learners want it).[9]

Achievement Goal Theory

Related to the Goal Setting Theory, the Achievement Goal Theory is used to explain why a student might be interested in completing a task. This theory offers two possible reasons for students to complete a goal. They are either mastery-oriented or performance-oriented. Mastery-oriented students are seeking to understand the content. Performance-oriented students are seeking to avoid failure or to outperform peers. Mastery orientation is obviously preferred.[10]

Herzberg's Two-Factor Theory

Herzberg's Two-Factor Theory also relates to motivation within the workplace. This theory offers two relevant types of factors: *motivators*, such as responsibility or recognition, which increase motivation; and *hygiene*, such as status or benefits, which when absent decrease motivation. Hygiene factors do not increase motivation by being present; it is only their lack that affects motivation negatively.[11]

Interest Theory

Interest Theory suggests that individuals are motivated by the interest that they have for an activity. Interest is developed within four stages. First, there is a triggered situational interest, followed by a sustained situational interest. Personal interest then follows, with an initial personal interest ending with a well-developed personal interest. Those with a personal interest in an activity are more likely to possess a higher motivation.[12]

Self-Determination Theory

Self-Determination Theory is a very influential and popular theory of motivation, which classifies motivation as either intrinsic or extrinsic. Intrinsic motivation is provided by an internal drive of interest, desire, or enjoyment. Extrinsic motivation is caused by an external influence, such as a reward or punishment. There are four types of extrinsic motivations within this theory that move along a sliding scale related to how self-determined the individual feels in relation to the influence. From least self-determined to most, the types of extrinsic motivation are External Regulation, Introjected Regulation, Identification, and Integration. The final type is then intrinsic, with the motivation being completely self-determined. Intrinsic motivation is the preferred type, with students learning due to an internal impetus.[13]

Motivational Models

While there are several theories of motivation, they share several strategies on how they can best be implemented in the classroom to help motivate students. Palmer offers a nice summary of the various motivation theories, their implications for instruction, and the corresponding teaching strategies that can be used to promote motivation, including facilitating success, novelty, choice, relevance, variety, social interaction, praise, encouragement, and teacher enthusiasm.[14] There are also more structured models that set out to provide practical application of the various theories within the classroom.

ARCS Model of Motivation

John Keller developed the ARCS Model of Motivation.[15] He sets out four prerequisites for student motivation as well as strategies to meet each. His four categories are (1) Attention, (2) Relevance, (3) Confidence, and (4) Satisfaction. This model is meant to provide a framework for setting up instruction in such a way as to motivate students.

MUSIC Model of Academic Motivation

The MUSIC Model of Academic Motivation was developed by Brett Jones in 2009.[16] It offers five components that can be used to motivate students: (1) eMpowerment, (2) Usefulness, (3) Success, (4) Interest, and (5) Caring. He notes that while these components may be used or discussed in other motivation theories, his theory is unique in that it combines the ideas into one entity that can be implemented by instructors within a classroom. His goal is to create a usable structure to help increase motivation.

Motivation in the Classroom

There is a point in the learning process when the content becomes unfamiliar and the learner becomes uncomfortable. This learning edge or liminal space is a critical time for students. If the content seems too advanced, or if learning the content seems not worth the effort required, students can shut down. They may throw up mental blocks, become frustrated, and be unwilling to progress. In some instances, these learning edges may occur around threshold concepts. This is due to the fact that threshold concepts are usually difficult or counterintuitive. The importance of these concepts cannot be denied, however, as their comprehension results in permanent change in the way the students understand the material being taught. Therefore, it is critical that instructors help students as they tackle these concepts. Successful instructors find ways to move students across that edge and into new territory where learning can occur.

Helping students in that liminal space is accomplished through motivation. Motivation is important because "when learners are motivated during the learning process, things go more smoothly, communication flows, anxiety decreases, and creativity and learning are more apparent."[17] Motivation is a critical component of students' success. Sankaran and Bui and Dunigan and Curry all found that high motivation correlated with high performance, while low motivation correlated with low performance in online courses.[18]

Motivation can be experienced in a number of forms. Brophy views the motivation to learn as either a temporary state or permanent trait: "Motivation as a Trait: An enduring disposition to value knowledge as a worthwhile and satisfying activity, a striving for knowledge and mastery in learning situations. Motivation as a State: A state of motivation guided by a goal or intention. Students reveal motivation to learn when they complete assignments or lessons."[19] Within any classroom, there will be a mix of students who possess motivation as an ingrained trait or as a temporary state. Those students for whom motivation is a trait can be a joy to instruct, as they push forward focused on the topic at hand. Those students for whom the motivation for learning is a state that can wax and wane may be harder to reach. However, as noted earlier, motivation is not a singularly established feature; it is possible to develop and promote the motivational growth of all students.

Motivation within Information Literacy Sessions

Information literacy encompasses skills and knowledge that aid individuals as they complete research both in and outside of the classroom; however, it is "wildly optimistic to assume that arguments linking IL with academic success will be sufficiently persuasive to all individuals."[20] Motivation to engage with the content offered in library information literacy instruction must often be provided by the librarian offering that instruction. When students reach a point where learning becomes difficult, it is up to the instructor to help motivate them to move through those challenges into the zone of understanding. Ambrose and colleagues state that "motivation refers to the personal investment made by an individual to reach a desired outcome."[21]

Pinto notes that a "fundamental question facing university communities is how to raise levels of motivation… on the critical issue of information literacy."[22] Designing instruction that incorporates motivation is especially important in the library instruction offered by librarians since they often meet with students only for single sessions. "Information educators often do not have as clearly defined a role as teachers, a situation that leaves them needing to demonstrate their value to students."[23] These sessions often occur with little external motivation within the larger course. Research skills that are discussed may be a part of a research paper within the course; however, unless the course faculty member stresses the importance of these skills, the students may skip over the research to focus more on the writing of the paper.

Thus, it is even more important for librarians to tap into the forces of internal motivation when providing instruction. Motivation within information literacy instruction has been addressed throughout the library literature. Jacobson and Xu discuss the importance of motivation in their article.[24] Many other authors note the importance of motivation and how intrinsic motivation connects deeply with information literacy:

- "Intrinsic motivation is at the core of information literacy, the foundation for a desire to learn and find information independently."[25]
- "Students with an intrinsic (or internal) orientation find satisfaction from simply participating in a learning experience that stimulates their curiosity and interest, promotes their feelings of competence or control, and/or is inherently pleasurable."[26]
- "The self-motivating, self-renewing dimensions of engaged learning go to the very core of lifelong learning, a concept often linked with information literacy."[27]

While it is acknowledged that intrinsic motivation insures that students will continue to apply themselves to problems, it is necessary to address a range of intrinsic and extrinsic motivations. During full-length semester classes it can be problematic to offer an extrinsic reward to students at the beginning of the semester and then continue it throughout the semester. If they are denied the reward, some students may give up the desired behavior.

Within a one-time instruction session, however, extrinsic motivations can be an effective method to quickly reach students. This is due to several characteristics of such an interaction. First, it can take time and a connection with students in order to develop ingrained intrinsic motivation. A fifty-minute session does not allow the time for such a development. Second, extrinsic motivators often lose their effectiveness when they are not continued. In the case of a single library session, there is no continuation; therefore, the impact cannot be reduced. Finally, extrinsic motivators can be a way to quickly draw the attention of students. Within a short time frame, it is critical to capture and keep the attention of students. "Extrinsic motivators are very powerful and can quickly get students to master new behaviors and modify their existing behaviors."[28] Thus, even within the often short sessions that librarians hold with students, it is possible to utilize a variety of motivating factors.

Ways to Promote Motivation

An important note with regard to motivation is the fact that even though every student possesses a different amount and even differing kinds of motivation, is it still possible to positively affect the motivation of each student. Motivation is something that can be enhanced and developed both through long-term focus and for short-term gain. There are a range of motivators that can affect a student's desire to learn. The list from Grossnickle in table 1.1 presents intrinsic and extrinsic motivators.

Table 1.1
Intrinsic and extrinsic motivators for students (Source: Donald R. Grossnickle, *Helping Students Develop Self-Motivation* [Reston, VA: National Association of Secondary School Principals, 1989], 6-7).

Intrinsic	Extrinsic
Making Choices	Influence
To Belong	Persuasion
Success	Status
Control	Goals
Interest	Guilt
Goals	Adult Approval (Teacher/Parent)
Creativity	Fear of Punishment
Self-Esteem	Interesting Activity
Career/Future	Avoid Blame
Guilt	Money
Games	Cooperation
Competence	Peer Approval
To Be Loved	Recognition/Acknowledgement
Overcome Obstacle/Handicap	Model/Example
Power	Praise
Relevancy/Perceived Utility	Gaining Privilege
Honor/Family Tradition	Coaxing
Challenge	
Encouragement/Coaching	
Acceptance	
Appreciation of Effort	
Curiosity/Suspense	
Enlightenment	
Good Attitude	
Competition	
Independence	
Duty/Obligation	
Cooperation	
Enjoyment	

There are a number of specific strategies that can also be used to promote motivation:

- Recognize and acknowledge student contributions.
- Explain or show why learning particular content or a particular skill is important.

- Allow students some opportunities to select learning goals and tasks.
- Create or maintain curiosity.
- Provide a variety of activities and sensory stimulations.
- Say thank you.
- Provide games and simulations.
- Use stories and examples.
- Connect learning to student values.
- Draw a connection between material and student's interest.
- Provide authentic problems or questions.
- Highlight new perspectives and diversity.
- Show enthusiasm.
- Provide opportunities for success early.
- Set goals for learning.
- Allow time to reflect.
- Relate learning to student needs.
- Provide clear expectations.
- Give corrective feedback.
- Provide valuable rewards for simple learning tasks.
- Make rewards available.
- Allow opportunities for students to observe more correct exemplars.
- Allow for opportunities to engage in social learning activities.
- Provide for scaffolding of corrective feedback.
- Help students develop plan of action.

Ways to Discourage Motivation

Just as it is important to have ideas on how to promote motivation, it is also helpful to understand actions that will negatively impact the motivation of students. Grossnickle offers a list of motivational pitfalls to avoid when attempting to develop self-motivation in students:

- faulty praise or patronizing
- use of fear and threats; punishment

- overuse of clichés ("no guts, no glory," etc.)
- shock value, overstating failure
- name calling, nagging, blaming, placing guilt
- put-downs, comparisons
- expecting too much or too little
- rationalizing failure, denying, making excuses
- ignoring or denying the warning signs of learning problems[29]

Motivational Influence within This Text

While the theoretical reasoning behind the motivating impact of the instructional techniques addressed in this book is influenced by several motivation theories, the idea of intrinsic and extrinsic motivation as described by the Self-Determination Theory merits special mention. Intrinsic motivation means that an action will be taken based on internal rather than external factors. Due to the personal nature of intrinsic motivation, Malone and Lepper go so far as to "use the words *fun, interesting, captivating, enjoyable,* and *intrinsically motivating* all more or less interchangeably."[30] Their research looks in depth into seven factors that promote intrinsic motivation: fantasy, challenge, competition, cooperation, recognition, control, and curiosity. They characterize these factors as individual or interpersonal. The individual factors are the following:

- **Challenge**—Individuals seek out and enjoy activities that they find challenging. To be challenging, the activity must possess a goal, uncertain outcomes, feedback on performance, and a connection to self-esteem.

- **Fantasy**—Fantasy appeals to two aspects of individuals' personalities: their emotional needs, which provide feelings that may not be experienced elsewhere, and cognitive aspects, which connect new information to a made-up situation.

- **Curiosity**—Curiosity can be understood in two ways: sensory curiosity, which attracts attention with sensory stimuli, and cognitive curiosity, which attracts attention by causing individuals to question their existing knowledge.

- **Control**—When they are provided with options and the chance to control their own choices, individuals are allowed to experience a more personal connection to the material.

The interpersonal factors are the following:

- **Cooperation**—A group of individuals are working together to achieve a common goal.
- **Competition**—A group of individuals, either singularly or in groups, are working to achieve a goal in which success for one results in a loss for another.
- **Recognition**—The results of an activity are visible to others throughout the process or in the product or result.

"Making an activity more intrinsically motivating to students may also have a profound influence on their cognitive involvement with the activity. Differences in cognitive involvement, in turn, may determine how information is processed and whether that knowledge can later be remembered or transferred to new problems."[31] These seven factors that encourage intrinsic motivation are addressed by the instructional techniques that will be presented in upcoming chapters.

Conclusion

Throughout all these differing theories of motivation, we see that motivation remains an important concept affecting the manner in which learning is approached. Motivation is something that can be enhanced, and as educators, librarians need to be aware of the techniques that will allow us to help our students as they face times of uncertainty in their learning. By providing the motivation for students on the learning edge as they confront threshold concepts, we will be able to guide them toward a more complete understanding of new material and concepts and ultimately the development of information literacy.

Notes

1. Morris Mandel, *A Complete Treasury of Stories for Public Speakers* (Middle Village, NY: Johnathan David Publishers, 1974).
2. Abraham H. Maslow, "A Theory of Human Motivation," *Psychological Review* 50, no. 4 (1943): 370–96.
3. Frits Helder, *The Psychology of Interpersonal Relations* (New York: Wiley, 1958).
4. J. Stacy Adams, "Towards an Understanding of Inequity," *Journal of Abnormal and Social Psychology* 67, no. 5 (1963): 422–36.
5. John W. Atkinson, "Motivational Determinants of Risk Taking Behavior," *Psychological Review* 64, no. 6, pt. 1 (November 1957): 359–72.
6. Ibid.

7. Albert Bandura, "Self-Efficacy: Toward a Unifying Theory of Behavioral Change," *Psychological Review* 84, no. 2 (1977): 193..
8. Martin V. Covington, "The Self-Worth Theory of Achievement Motivation: Findings and Implications," *Elementary School Journal* 85, no. 1 (1984): 4–20.
9. Barbara L. McCombs and James E. Pope, *Motivating Hard to Reach Students,* Psychology in the Classroom Series (Washington, DC: American Psychological Association, 1994); Edwin A. Locke and Gary P. Latham, *A Theory of Goal Setting and Task Performance* (Englewood Cliffs, NJ: Prentice Hall, 1990).
10. Carol S. Dweck, "Motivational Aspects Affecting Learning," *American Psychologist* 41, no. 10 (1986): 1040–48.
11. Frederick Herzberg, "One More Time: How Do You Motivate Employees?" *Harvard Business Review* 46, no. 1 (1968): 53–62.
12. K. Ann Renninger, Lore Hoffmann, and Andreas Krapp, "Interest and Gender: Issues of Development and Learning," in *Interest and Learning: Proceedings of the Second Conference on Interest and Learning,* ed. Lore Hoffmann, Andreas Krapp, K. Ann Renninger, and Jürgen Baumert (Kiel, Germany: IPN, 1998), 9–21.
13. Edward L. Deci and Richard M. Ryan, "The 'What' and 'Why' of Goal Pursuits: Human Needs and the Self-Determination of Behavior," *Psychological Inquiry* 11, no. 4 (2000): 227–68.
14. David Palmer, "What Is the Best Way to Motivate Students in Science?" *Teaching Science* 53, no. 1 (2007): 38–42.
15. John Keller, *Motivational Design for Learning and Performance* (New York: Springer, 2009).
16. Brett Jones, "Motivating Students to Engage in Learning: The MUSIC Model of Academic Motivation," *International Journal of Teaching and Learning in Higher Education* 21, no. 2 (2009): 272–85.
17. Raymond J. Wlodkowski, *Enhancing Adult Motivation to Learn* (San Francisco: Jossey-Bass, 1985), 4.
18. Siva R. Sankaran and Tung Bui, "Impact of Learning Strategies and Motivation on Performance: A Study in Web-Based Instruction," *Journal of Instructional Psychology* 28, no. 3 (2001): 191–98; Beth Dunigan and Kenneth J. Curry, "Motivation and Learning Strategies of Students in Distance Education," *Journal of the Mississippi Academy of Sciences* 51, no. 2 (2006): 140–55.
19. Jere Brophy, *Socializing Student Motivation to Learn,* Institute for Research in Teaching, Published Monograph, Research Series 169 (East Lansing: College of Education, Michigan State University, 1986), quoted in Grossnickle, *Helping Students Develop,* 2.
20. Andrew K. Shenton and Megan Fitzgibbons, "Making Information Literacy Relevant," *Library Review* 59, no. 3 (2010): 165.
21. Susan A. Ambrose, Michael Bridges, Michelle DiPietro, Marsha Lovett, and Marie Norman, *How Learning Works* (San Francisco: Jossey-Bass, 2010), 68.
22. Maria Pinto, "An Approach to the Internal Facet of Information Literacy Using the IL-HUMASS Survey," *Journal of Academic Librarianship* 37, no. 2 (2011): 146.
23. Shenton and Fitzgibbons, "Making Information Literacy Relevant," 170.
24. Trudi E. Jacobson and Lijuan Xu, "Motivating Students in Credit-Based Information Literacy Courses: Theories and Practice," *portal: Libraries and the Academy* 2, no. 3 (2002): 423–41.
25. Sherry R. Crow, "Information Literacy: What's Motivation Got to Do with It?" *Knowledge Quest* 35, no. 4 (2007): 52.

26. Ruth V. Small, Nasriah Zakaria, and Houria El-Figuigui, "Motivational Aspects of Information Literacy Skills Instruction in Community College Libraries," *College and Research Libraries* 65, no. 2 (2004): 99.

27. Craig Gibson, ed., *Student Engagement and Information Literacy* (Chicago: Association of College and Research Libraries, 2006), x.

28. Trudi E. Jacobson and Lijuan Xu, *Motivating Students in Information Literacy Classes* (New York: Neal-Schuman, 2004), 5.

29. Grossnickle, *Helping Students Develop*, 7.

30. Thomas W. Malone and Mark R. Lepper, "Making Learning Fun: A Taxonomy of Intrinsic Motivations for Learning," in *Aptitude, Learning, and Instruction: Conative and Affective Process Analyses*, ed. Richard E. Snow and Marshall J. Farr (Hillsdale, NJ: Lawrence Erlbaum Associates, 1987), 229.

31. Mark R. Lepper and Thomas W. Malone, "Intrinsic Motivation and Instructional Effectiveness in Computer-Based Education," in *Aptitude, Learning, and Instruction: Conative and Affective Process Analyses*, ed. Richard E. Snow and Marshall J. Farr (Hillsdale, NJ: Lawrence Erlbaum Associates, 1987), 270.

Bibliography

Adams, J. Stacy. "Towards an Understanding of Inequity." *Journal of Abnormal and Social Psychology* 67, no. 5 (1963): 422–36.

Ambrose, Susan A., Michael Bridges, Michelle DiPietro, Marsha Lovett, and Marie Norman. *How Learning Works: Seven Research-Based Principles for Smart Teaching*. San Francisco: Jossey-Bass, 2010.

Atkinson, John W. "Motivational Determinants of Risk Taking Behavior." *Psychological Review* 64, no. 6, pt. 1 (November 1957): 359–72.

Bandura, Albert. "Self-Efficacy: Toward a Unifying Theory of Behavioral Change." *Psychological Review* 84, no. 2 (1977): 191–215.

Brophy, Jere. *Socializing Student Motivation to Learn*. Institute for Research in Teaching, Published Monograph, Research Series 169. East Lansing: College of Education, Michigan State University, 1986.

Covington, Martin V. "The Self-Worth Theory of Achievement Motivation: Findings and Implications." *Elementary School Journal* 85, no. 1 (1984): 4–20.

Crow, Sherry R. "Information Literacy: What's Motivation Got to Do with It?" *Knowledge Quest* 35, no. 4 (2007): 48–52.

Deci, Edward L., and Richard M. Ryan. "The 'What' and 'Why' of Goal Pursuits: Human Needs and the Self-Determination of Behavior." *Psychological Inquiry* 11, no. 4 (2000): 227–68.

Dunigan, Beth, and Kenneth J. Curry. "Motivation and Learning Strategies of Students in Distance Education." *Journal of the Mississippi Academy of Sciences* 51, no. 2 (2006): 140–55.

Dweck, Carol. S. "Motivational Aspects Affecting Learning." *American Psychologist* 41, no. 10 (1986.): 1040–48.

Gibson, Craig, ed. *Student Engagement and Information Literacy*. Chicago: Association of College and Research Libraries, 2006.

Grossnickle, Donald R. *Helping Students Develop Self-Motivation: A Sourcebook for Parents and Educators*. Reston, VA: National Association of Secondary School Principals, 1989.

Helder, Frits. *The Psychology of Interpersonal Relations.* New York: Wiley, 1958.

Herzberg, Frederick. "One More Time: How Do You Motivate Employees?" *Harvard Business Review* 46, no. 1 (1968): 53–62.

Jacobson, Trudi E., and Lijuan Xu. "Motivating Students in Credit-Based Information Literacy Courses: Theories and Practice." *portal: Libraries and the Academy* 2, no. 3 (2002): 423–41.

———. *Motivating Students in Information Literacy Classes.* New York: Neal-Schuman, 2004.

Jones, Brett. "Motivating Students to Engage in Learning: The MUSIC Model of Academic Motivation." *International Journal of Teaching and Learning in Higher Education* 21, no. 2 (2009): 272–85.

Keller, John. *Motivational Design for Learning and Performance: The ARCS Model Approach.* New York: Springer, 2009.

Lepper, Mark R., and Thomas W. Malone. "Intrinsic Motivation and Instructional Effectiveness in Computer-Based Education." In *Aptitude, Learning, and Instruction: Conative and Affective Process Analyses.* Edited by Richard E. Snow and Marshall J. Farr, 255–86. Hillsdale, NJ: Lawrence Erlbaum Associates, 1987.

Locke, Edwin A., and Gary P. Latham. *A Theory of Goal Setting and Task Performance.* Englewood Cliffs, NJ: Prentice Hall, 1990.

Malone, Thomas W., and Mark R. Lepper. "Making Learning Fun: A Taxonomy of Intrinsic Motivations for Learning." In *Aptitude, Learning, and Instruction: Conative and Affective Process Analyses.* Edited by Richard E. Snow and Marshall J. Farr, 223–53. Hillsdale, NJ: Lawrence Erlbaum Associates, 1987.

Mandel, Morris. *A Complete Treasury of Stories of Stories for Public Speakers.* Middle Village, N.Y.: Johnathan David Publishers, 1974.

Maslow, Abraham H. "A Theory of Human Motivation." *Psychological Review* 50, no. 4 (1943): 370–96.

McCombs, Barbara L., and James E. Pope. *Motivating Hard to Reach Students.* Psychology in the Classroom Series. Washington, DC: American Psychological Association, 1994.

Palmer, David. "What Is the Best Way to Motivate Students in Science?" *Teaching Science* 53, no. 1 (2007): 38–42.

Pinto, Maria. "An Approach to the Internal Facet of Information Literacy Using the IL-HUMASS Survey." *Journal of Academic Librarianship* 37, no. 2 (2011): 145–54.

Renninger, K. Ann, Lore Hoffmann, and Andreas Krapp. "Interest and Gender: Issues of Development and Learning." In *Interest and Learning: Proceedings of the Second Conference on Interest and Learning.* Edited by Lore Hoffmann, Andreas Krapp, K. Ann Renninger, and Jürgen Baumert, 9–21. Kiel, Germany: IPN, 1998.

Sankaran, Siva R., and Tung Bui. "Impact of Learning Strategies and Motivation on Performance: A Study in Web-Based Instruction." *Journal of Instructional Psychology* 28, no. 3 (2001): 191–98.

Shenton, Andrew K., and Megan Fitzgibbons. "Making Information Literacy Relevant." *Library Review* 59, no. 3 (2010): 165–74.

Small, Ruth V., Nasriah Zakaria, and Houria El-Figuigui. "Motivational Aspects of Information Literacy Skills Instruction in Community College Libraries." *College and Research Libraries* 65, no. 2 (2004): 96–121.

Wlodkowski, Raymond J. *Enhancing Adult Motivation to Learn.* San Francisco: Jossey-Bass, 1985.

CHAPTER 2

Fun as a Means of Motivation

Although students don't always know where Fun sits, they all know where Rigor sits, and few willingly sit near him. Rigor can feel isolated, unwanted, disconsolate. When Rigor feels that way, there is danger of him becoming supercilious. After all, Rigor sees himself as exclusive, demanding, and difficult. To keep perspective, Rigor needs the companionship of Fun. And Fun, of course, benefits from the company of Rigor. In fact, Fun and Rigor are each at their best when they collaborate to produce something together that neither could create alone. That's when they entertain their mutual best friend, Fulfillment.[1]

What Is Fun?

Ask a large group of people what they do for fun; their responses will be all over the map. Then ask that group why their response is fun. The answers will now fall into very specific themes with some common words appearing over and over. "I enjoy it." "It amuses me." "It makes me happy." Going through a list of all the definitions, synonyms, and examples of fun, one finds a string of positives. Fun is something that is so common and so often discussed that we rarely consider its definition. It ends up being one of those things that "we know when we see it." However, a common understanding will be necessary throughout this text. To that end, *fun* is defined as **that which causes enjoyment, amusement, or pleasure.**

While fun and motivation are the focus of this work and have been defined, another term that often occurs in the research literature, especially in relation to motivation, is *engagement*. The lesson plans in part II aim to use instructional techniques that are fun as a motivating force in order to encourage students to engage with the content of the lesson. Engagement with instructional content is the goal of the lesson plans, as it is through this engagement that students will be able to interact with and internalize the content. It is possible to engage with content without the use of fun, but these instructional techniques that include fun are aimed at providing additional motivation for student engagement.

Fun in Education

According to Bryant, Comisky, and Zillmann, fun did not have a place in the earliest organized colleges, due to the fact that students paid their teachers directly in order to get instruction focused specifically on the topic. There were restrictions "dictating that the professor strictly had to follow the text, explain difficult problems, and cover a specified amount of material during each term."[2] There was no time for frivolous fun within education. Acceptance of fun into education has taken years, but now the idea of fun is viewed favorably within elementary through high school contexts. However, there still remains a small stigma against fun within parts of higher education. For some, school is a serious undertaking and should be treated as such. Some professors see the introduction of fun as the start down a slippery slope of lost respectability. For if the students are laughing in class, how can they respect either the professor or the content?

Another negative in the case for fun within education is the tendency to conflate fun with entertainment. Yes, entertainment also causes enjoyment, amusement, and pleasure, but just because a cat and a dog both have ears, tongue, and teeth does not mean that they are the same thing. Ask any dog lover or cat fancier, and they will let you know about the difference.

The judicious use of fun within the classroom does not mean that the focus of the instruction is on providing entertainment. The instructor is still an instructor, which means the focus is on instruction, and more importantly, on learning. Rigor is not to be compromised when applying fun. To the contrary, fun can be used as one means of increasing the rigor. Fun is often viewed as an auxiliary component, perhaps as a way to break the ice, but not as a true factor in instruction. However, fun can also be a successful method of connecting students with content. As Mathers states, "Fun and hard work do not have to be mutually exclusive; rather, fun may actually encourage higher levels of engagement and effort."[3] For if the classroom includes fun and causes the students to experience enjoyment, amusement, or pleasure, they will be more engaged in the content, which allows them to experience deeper learning.

Fun also results in the creation of an environment that promotes immediacy. Immediacy is the ability to convey to others both through verbal and nonverbal means that someone is open to communicating and interacting with others. This openness on the part of an instructor enhances student-teacher interaction. Potee describes verbal and nonverbal methods that promote immediacy. Those methods that are highlighted in the instructional techniques found in this book include openness, friendliness, and smiling.[4]

Students agree that they would like to experience fun as part of their college courses. In a study of college students, Strage found that the top characteristics of an "ideal" professor included knowledgeable (46.8%), caring and concerned about their students (44.2%), and funny/entertaining (40.2%). The top characteristics of the "ideal" course were engaging (53.6%) and fun (27.1%).[5]

The use of fun in the classroom is not only a complement to learning, but according to Dörnyei, the lack of fun may actually be a detriment: "Boring but systematic teaching can be effective in getting short-term results, but rarely does it inspire a lifelong commitment to the subject matter."[6] Fun provides a means of motivating students. The level of motivation students have for a task is one way to determine academic proficiency, engagement, and persistence. Motivated "learners also may be more willing to select tasks at the border of their competencies."[7] This means that by motivating students through fun, it is possible to also engage them with more challenging educational content.

Fun in the Library

Depending on one's past experiences and situation in life, the heading for this section either makes perfect sense or is completely incomprehensible. Since most readers will be librarians, it is likely that they will relate to the former. But as librarians also know, there are a number of individuals who do not share such a positive relationship with libraries.

And while some may be able to connect fun to certain aspects of the library, such as checking out DVDs and bestselling novels, fun is often not considered to be a feature of the information literacy instruction offered by librarians. Librarians face the same quandaries as other faculty members when deciding whether to use fun within their classes. They may also feel additional pressure to highlight the serious, critically important aspect of their content due to the fact that information literacy is so often misunderstood and considered of secondary importance. If you do not feel confident in your position as an instructor, it is hard to have fun within that role.

There is indication that some librarians do accept the use of fun within the educational context. As part of an online survey I conducted in 2013, 266 librarians with instructional responsibilities responded to the statements shown in figures 2.1, 2.2, and 2.3 related to learning, fun, and challenge.

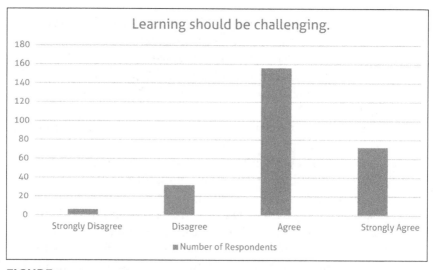

FIGURE 2.1

Responses to the statement "Learning should be challenging."

When stating their degree of agreement with the statement "Learning should be challenging," 6 respondents (2%) said Strongly Disagree, 32 respondents (12%) said Disagree, 156 respondents (59%) said Agree, and 72 respondents (27%) said Strongly Agree.

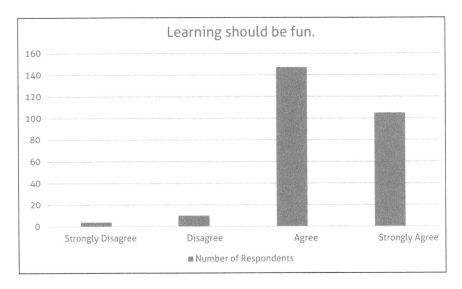

FIGURE 2.2

Responses to the statement "Learning should be fun."

Responding to the statement "Learning should be fun," 4 respondents (2%) said Strongly Disagree, 10 respondents (4%) said Disagree, 147 respondents (55%) said Agree, and 105 respondents (39%) said Strongly Agree.

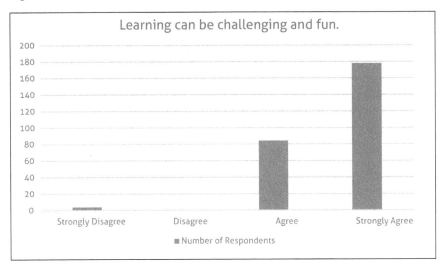

FIGURE 2.3

Responses to the statement "Learning can be challenging and fun."

Finally, given the statement "Learning can be challenging and fun," 4 respondents (2%) said Strongly Disagree, 0 respondents (0%) said Disagree, 84 respondents (32%) said Agree, and 178 (67%) said Strongly Agree.

Instruction librarians focus on helping students develop the skills and knowledge associated with information literacy. This instructional goal requires methods of engaging students and helping them cross the learning edge so that they are able to form a connection with the subject matter being presented. Looking at instruction through the lens of fun provides useful opportunities to facilitate these connections.

Instructional Techniques

Instruction is a major responsibility of many librarians. Whether librarians are offering for-credit courses or providing instruction on the fly at the reference desk, teaching others about information in its many facets is a critical skill required by almost all librarians. Few librarians, however, receive specific training on how to teach. They may rely on their own experiences as students or suggestions from others in developing their teaching style and techniques.

In considering how instructional techniques are developed, one place to begin would be with instructional strategies; these are "the overall planned procedures for implementing and achieving specific goals and objectives in teaching."[8] To have a successful instructional strategy, various teaching methods must be utilized. Methods of instruction include a mix of **materials, exercises,** and **techniques.** In this organizational scheme, **materials** are objects utilized by students, such as textbooks; **exercises** are requirements the students must undertake, for example, completing a worksheet; and **techniques** are the ways in which the students interact with the content, for example, listening to a lecture. Instructional techniques are a systematic way of making knowledge available to students.

When considering instruction, it is important to take a look at the instructional techniques used to teach students. Mokhtar, Majid, and Foo note, "More often than not, what and the amount that students learn is greatly shaped by the way that they are taught. In other words, the manner in which students are taught, in addition to the information and factual content, will somehow influence the quantity and quality of what is learnt and retained."[9]

Instructional Techniques That Include Fun

Given the positive impact that fun can have upon education, one must therefore consider which instructional techniques meet the definition of fun, **that which causes enjoyment, amusement, or pleasure.** In looking at lists of various instructional techniques that might be included in this book, I focused on those techniques that are student-centered and that address the above definition of fun. While it is possible to make the case for other instructional techniques to be included, the instructional techniques involving fun that will be presented in this book are **humor, games**, and **group work**. These three techniques provide a systematic means of promoting student motivation while at the same time meeting our definition of fun. The focus on conscious consideration and application of these techniques is an important component of this book. Care and thought must be used when determining what content to provide for students as well as how that content will be presented and how the students will be encouraged to engage with it.

Humor clearly fits within the definition of fun as it is meant to cause **amusement** or laughter. Often one of the physical characteristics that can be seen when a group or individual is having fun is the sharing of laughter. In this book, humor relates specifically to amusement or laughter resulting from a cognitive function. So while there may be laughter coming from a Silly Silo, this is not the humor that should be found within the classroom. Humor requires active engagement with the mind, resulting in fun that fits well within the purview of education. Korobkin, Vossler and Sheidlower, and Berk all provide valid reasons for incorporating humor into the classroom.[10]

As the next instructional technique, **games** are also readily recognized as fun. Games are often used by individuals or groups as a **pleasurable** activity. This pleasure is what keeps players coming back to a game. Games require a set structure of rules and guidelines that allow an individual player or players to reach a final goal. Games are receiving more and more attention in education as a means of providing educational content, with over 2,300 results found in a search in ERIC between 2013 and 2016 alone. Instructors are tapping into students' predisposition toward and enjoyment of games as well as the wide range of implementation options in order to cover a variety of topics within the classroom.

Group work is the last instructional technique discussed in this book, and the one which may cause the most disagreement with regard to its connection with fun. This would stem from the fact that a number of individuals have experienced group work in a class with negative results. This, however, was not the fault of group work itself, but rather in the way it was implemented. There are a number of parameters that must be put in place for group work to be successful.[11] Group work requires individuals working together to reach a common goal. When the parameters are in place and everyone in the group is able to contribute, even an introverted individual can take part and **enjoy** working with a group. Successful groups have been shown at all levels to improve learning and thus can potentially be a major instructional technique that uses fun to add to classroom instruction.[12]

Conclusion

Fun creates a motivational environment where connections are possible within the classroom. A positive environment that includes fun allows students to connect with the instructor; fun can also grab students' attention and allow them to connect with the content. And finally, the shared experience allows the students to connect with each other. The sum of all these connections is a feeling of connection with the library itself. These positive experiences lead to greater and more productive use of the library in the future.

When one considers the idea of "fun" as that which causes enjoyment, amusement, and pleasure, it can easily be connected to education. Fun is not to be confused with something that is easy. Fun is to be connected with rigorous content. This connection is important, as it provides a means of assisting students in an understanding of the content by providing the motivation to encourage active engagement with the material. By using fun as a motivational tool to help students work through content that may be difficult or confusing, librarians will be able to move students over the learning edge into an understanding and internalization of threshold concepts.

Notes

1.   Tom Romano, "Defining Fun and Seeking Flow in English Language Arts," *English Journal* 98, no. 6 (2009): 36.
2.   Jennings Bryant, Paul Comisky, and Dolf Zillmann, "Teachers' Humor in the College Classroom," *Communication Education* 28, no. 2 (1979): 110.
3.   Brandi Gribble Mathers, "Students' Perceptions of 'Fun' Suggest Possibilities for Literacy Learning: 'You Can be Entertained and Informed,'" *Reading Horizons* 49, no. 1 (2008): 81.
4.   Nanette Potee, "Teacher Immediacy and Student Motivation," in *Sociocultural Influ-*

ences on Motivation and Learning: An Historical Perspective, ed. Dennis M. McIner-ney and Shawn Van Etten (Greenwich, CT: Information Age, 2002), 211.

5.   Amy Strage, "Traditional and Non-traditional College Students' Descriptions of the 'Ideal' Professor and the 'Ideal' Course and Perceived Strengths and Limitations," *College Student Journal* 42, no. 1 (2008): 225–31.

6.   Dörnyei, Zoltan, *Teaching and Researching Motivation* (Essex, UK: Pearson, 2001). as cited in Manuela Wagner and Edwardo Urios-Aparisi, "The Use of Humor in the Foreign Language Classroom: Funny and Effective?" *Humor* 24, no. 4 (2011): 406.

7.   Kirby Deater-Deckard, Mido Chang, and Michael E. Evans, "Engagement State and Learning from Educational Games," in *Digital Games: A Context for Cognitive Development,* New Directions for Child and Adolescent Development 139, ed. Fran C. Blumber and Shalom M. Fisch (San Francisco: Jossey Bass, 2013), 22.

8.   John W. Collins and Patricia O'Brien, eds., *The Greenwood Dictionary of Education* (Westport, CT: Greenwood Press, 2003), s.v. "instructional strategies."

9.   Intan Azura Mokhtar, Shaheen Majid, and Schubert Foo, "Teaching Information Literacy through Learning Styles: The Application of Gardner's Multiple Intelligences," *Journal of Librarianship and Information Science* 40, no. 2 (2008): 95.

10.   Debra Korobkin, "Humor in the Classroom," *College Teaching* 36, no. 4 (1988): 154–58; Joshua Vossler and Scott Sheidlower, *Humor and Information Literacy* (Santa Barbara, CA: Libraries Unlimited, 2011); Ronald Berk, *Humor as an Instructional Defibrillator* (Sterling, VA: Stylus Publishing, 2002).

11.   Chet Meyers and Thomas B. Jones, *Promoting Active Learning Strategies for the College Classroom* (San Francisco: Jossey-Bass, 1993).

12.   David W. Johnson, Roger T. Johnson, and Mary Beth Stanne, "Cooperative Learning Methods: A Meta-Analysis," Cooperative Learning Center at the University of Minnesota, May 2000, http://www.clcrc.com/pages/cl-methods.html (site now discontinued).

Bibliography

Berk, Ronald. *Humor as an Instructional Defibrillator.* Sterling, VA: Stylus Publishing, 2002.

Bryant, Jennings, Paul Comisky, and Dolf Zillmann. "Teachers' Humor in the College Classroom." *Communication Education* 28, no. 2 (1979): 110–18.

Collins, John W., and Patricia O'Brien, eds. *The Greenwood Dictionary of Education.* Westport, CT: Greenwood Press, 2003.

Deater-Deckard, Kirby, Mido Chang, and Michael E. Evans. "Engagement State and Learning from Educational Games." In *Digital Games: A Context for Cognitive Development.* New Directions for Child and Adolescent Development 139. Edited by Fran C. Blumber and Shalom M. Fisch, 21–30. San Francisco: Jossey Bass, 2013.

Johnson, David W., Roger T. Johnson, and Mary Beth Stanne. "Cooperative Learning Methods: A Meta-Analysis." Cooperative Learning Center at the University of Minnesota, May 2000. http://www.clcrc.com/pages/cl-methods.html (site now discontinued).

Korobkin, Debra. "Humor in the Classroom." *College Teaching* 36, no. 4 (1988): 154–58.

Mathers, Brandi Gribble. "Students' Perceptions of 'Fun' Suggest Possibilities for Literacy Learning: 'You Can Be Entertained and Informed.'" *Reading Horizons* 49, no. 1 (2008): 71–88.

Meyers, Chet, and Thomas B. Jones. *Promoting Active Learning Strategies for the College Classroom*. San Francisco: Jossey-Bass, 1993.

Mokhtar, Intan Azura, Shaheen Majid, and Schubert Foo. "Teaching Information Literacy through Learning Styles: The Application of Gardner's Multiple Intelligences." *Journal of Librarianship and Information Science* 40, no. 2 (2008): 93–109.

Potee, Nanette. "Teacher Immediacy and Student Motivation." In *Sociocultural Influences on Motivation and Learning: An Historical Perspective*. Edited by Dennis M. McInerney and Shawn Van Etten, 207–24. Greenwich, CT: Information Age, 2002.

Romano, Tom. "Defining Fun and Seeking Flow in English Language Arts." *English Journal* 98, no. 6 (2009): 30–37.

Strage, Amy. "Traditional and Non-traditional College Students' Descriptions of the 'Ideal' Professor and the 'Ideal' Course and Perceived Strengths and Limitations." *College Student Journal* 42, no. 1 (2008): 225–31.

Vossler, Joshua, and Scott Sheidlower. *Humor and Information Literacy: Practical Techniques for Library Instruction*. Santa Barbara, CA: Libraries Unlimited, 2011.

Wagner, Manuela, and Edwardo Urios-Aparisi. "The Use of Humor in the Foreign Language Classroom: Funny and Effective?" *Humor* 24, no. 4 (2011): 399–434.

CHAPTER 3

Humor

Humor is an invitation to think differently, from another perspective, while at the same time inhabiting one's own perspective; in other words, humor encourages one to learn.[1]

The use of humor in the classroom is probably one of the most recognizable illustrations of fun in education. Imagine a hallway with classrooms along each side. You can hear the voices of the faculty as they lecture the students and the indistinguishable mumble as a student answers a question. Then from one room comes the sound of several voices joined together in laughter. You instinctively think, it sounds like they are having fun, and your curiosity is aroused, wondering what that class is talking about, what subject they are discussing, and what you can do to join in. Humor is a universal positive. All ages and cultures utilize humor, starting with the first baby laughing for the first time. The positive effects of humor spread throughout a group as that laugh breaks into a thousand pieces.

What Is Humor?

While the *Oxford English Dictionary* lists multiple uses of the word *humor* stemming from multiple origins as far back as 1340, this book will utilize a definition found within Wikipedia that is applied in studies such as Singh, Tripathi, and Kohli.[2] This definition states, humor is **the tendency of particular cognitive experiences to provoke laughter or provide amusement**. Thus, the very nature of humor requires a cognitive reaction.

As instructors, we are focused primarily on connecting to students' cognitive functions, so anything that helps stimulate that connection should be considered for inclusion within our instruction.

There are a range of theories on humor. Three of the most highly referenced are **relief theory**, **superiority theory**, and **incongruity theory**. According to relief theory, humor is caused by an alleviation of tension. Superiority theory holds that humor is felt when we are able to feel superior to an individual or situation. Incongruity theory holds that humor is caused when we see the difference between what is happening and what should be happening.

Benefits of Humor in General

Before looking at how humor can be used in the classroom, let us first take a look at the benefits of humor within daily life. Humor and its by-product, laughter, have been studied by a range of disciplines. Martin, McGhee, and Provine all note that many of these studies may have methodical flaws due to small sample numbers;[3] however, given the number of studies that have been done and the persistent interest in humor as a topic of research, it is germane that we look at these studies in more depth. The benefits of humor discussed in these studies are both physiological and psychological.

Physiological

The **physiological benefits** are focused on the effect of humor on the physical body. These include a wide range of results. Some of the most basic describe how laughter can improve respiration and circulation. Laughter has been shown to exercise the chest, lungs, diaphragm, face, and stomach muscles. For anyone who has experienced a doubled-over, breathtaking, tear-inducing belly laugh, none of these results should come as a surprise. Laugher also results in more oxygen being put into the blood and a lowering of pulse and blood pressure. A laugh may not provide the same health benefits as regular exercise, but it will provide a nice in-between-gym-visits experience.

Humor and laughter also provide physical benefits that are not as readily seen or felt. The medical field has long noted the positive physical effects of humor and laughter, with articles discussing how it can be used when treating patients as well as its effects on medical school students.[4] There have been studies examining the release of endorphins into the bloodstream during laughter. Berk and Nanda note that laughter positively affects neuroendocrine and stress hormones.[5] Berk provides a review of a number of articles looking at the varied physical benefits of humor. These include improving mental functioning, exercising and relaxing muscles, improving respiration, stimulating circulation, decreasing stress hormones, increasing immune system defenses, and increasing pain threshold and tolerance.[6]

Psychological

The **psychological benefits** of humor relate to mental and emotional effects. Berk offers a list of eight psychological benefits of humor. Five lessen negative reactions through reducing anxiety, tension, stress, depression and loneliness, while three promote positive reactions through improving self-esteem, restoring hope and energy, and providing a sense of empowerment and control.[7]

Humor is one way to defuse tense situations. It can be a way to cause a short distraction, thereby allowing individuals to refocus on a new topic. This trick has been used for years by parents who make funny faces at crying babies or say something silly to an upset child. This tactic continues through adulthood. How often have we been in confrontational meetings that have been calmed down by someone providing a lighthearted comment? These injections of humor often provoke larger laughs than they would receive in a less stressful situation as the contrast between the situation and comment presents a greater degree of difference. There is also often a desire by those involved to have a break from the tension; therefore, they will eagerly and enthusiastically respond to any attempt to impose humor.

Humor also promotes creativity by stimulating the same areas of the brain that are used for reasoning and creative thinking. This can be illustrated clearly when a joke is told. *How many librarians does it take to change a light bulb?* After hearing this question, we are first cued that it will have a humorous reply in that it relies on a well-known joke format. Our interest is piqued as we start to consider what the reply may be. We may first search our memory for any instance of having heard this joke before. Then we start brainstorming possible answers. *One. We are librarians after all, and capable of anything.* True, but not really humorous. We also use our experiences with the content to come up a reply. *One librarian and seven board members to convince the city to raise the utilities budget.* Through our experiences with jokes, we start considering puns or turns of phrase that may fit. *535. The Dewey Decimal classification for light.* This understanding of language pushes our creativity even more as we try juxtaposing possible answers with humorous phrases. During this time, we are also in a heightened state of interest as we await the eventual punchline. This desire for a resolution is an important component of how humans respond to humor. So how many librarians does it take to change a light bulb? *I'm not sure, but I'll be happy to help you research that.* After the joke finishes, there is a relaxation of tension, and the audience is able to respond. Whether the response is an out-loud laugh, small smile, or exasperated groan, the steps of critical thinking and mental stimulation will have occurred.

Humor also can be used as a means to promote group unity. This occurs in a variety of ways. First, when sharing in humor and responding with laughter, a group is able to form a connection from the recognition that others found the same thing funny. This shared experience can be built upon later. Humor also results in a decrease of tension, allowing for groups to open up to one another. Responding to humor also lets members of the group view each other in a positive, open way. Looking around a room seeing other smiling, laughing faces encourages connection between individuals and lets them know that they can share with others.

Humor in the Classroom
Research Studies

Given the benefits of humor, it makes sense to incorporate it into classroom instruction whenever possible. A variety of positive results have been presented by individuals on the use of humor in education. Five uses suggested by Korobkin are promotion of a humanistic, laughter-filled learning environment; cultivation of group humor and group identification; promotion of self-discovery and risk-taking; development of retention cues; and release of anxiety and stress.[8] Vossler and Sheidlower note eight reasons for using humor in instruction: expressing personality, establishing trust, improving delivery and apparent competence, reducing student anxiety, gaining and maintaining student attention, fighting instructor burnout, promoting understanding and information retention, and undermining negative library or librarian stereotypes.[9] Berk notes how the benefits of humor can impact five areas of the classroom: professor-student connection, classroom atmosphere, student responsiveness, test performance, and student attendance.[10]

There have been numerous studies examining the effects of humor within the classroom. These results have been varied in impact and effectiveness, as they consider a wide range of uses of humor and approaches to using humor. Benefits of humor are shown to include students being more likely to retain content, students perceiving they learn more, increasing classroom rapport, defusing tense situations, contributing to increased creativity and divergent thinking, increasing student motivation, and providing stress relief.[11] Kher, Molstad, and Donahue suggests that humor has a place in "dread courses" that students avoid due to perceived difficulty, negative experience, or lack of confidence.[12] A survey by White notes that students felt that humor helped to explain complicated material, to motivate students, to relieve stress, to regain attention, to encourage participation, and to enable students to remember the content.[13] Physiologically "humor and laughter can aid learning through improved respiration and circulation, lower pulse and blood pressure, exercise of the chest muscles, greater oxygenation of blood, and the release of endorphins into the bloodstream."[14] There has been some question as to the ability of humor to improve learning, with some studies finding no improvement with the use of humor. Banas and colleagues provide a nice literature review of humor used in educational settings and note that "although the research assessing the impact of humor on actual learning is rather mixed, there is substantial empirical evidence that humor can enhance recall and aid learning."[15]

Within the library, humor may serve an additional purpose, as library anxiety may further hinder the learning of students who are already experiencing stress due to their coursework. Humor is an excellent method to help defuse that anxiety. Berk and Nanda show student anxiety decreased due to the use of humor.[16] "Library anxiety and stress can be reduced as students become more comfortable with the library's many resources."[17]

Some of the ways in which humor is especially important in developing motivation in the classroom is its ability to promote student-teacher connection and its ability to engage the students. A number of articles and essays detailing the use of humor in the classroom note its important role in attracting and maintaining the attention of the students. For many, this is the main obstacle when facing a group of students. Librarians often face students without the time to develop the same personal connections as their course instructors. They also lack the power of a grade to motivate the students to listen. Finally, they are often talking about a topic (research) that students have no interest in or feel that they already know how to do. Given the ability of humor to catch the attention of students, it would be wise to use it to its fullest capacity.

Humor and Technology

Humor intersects with technology in various ways. The first is that technology can be the means to provide humor, such as through a video. Humor also comes into play when using technology to offer instructional content to students at a distance. When offering instruction online, humor can be used as a means to humanize the content. James provides a call for the conscientious inclusion of humor within online classes.[18] Without the personalized contact found in a classroom, online students can experience a dwindling motivation to engage with the content. Imlawi and Gregg looked at how online social networks can increase student engagement when instructors share content-related personal details as well as humor.[19]

There have also been studies looking at the effectiveness of humor within online environments. Kobler and Nitzschner found that a funny YouTube video resulted in better understanding of a concept over a serious YouTube video and Wikipedia article.[20] Basamak and Mahiroglu found use of humor to increase student success in an online course.[21]

When interacting with students during online instruction, special consideration should be given to understanding. Since written language lacks the vocal variations that signal students to the fact you are being funny, it is important to either avoid unclear language or provide a cue that your comment was humorous. A common emoticon or "lol" can signal your humorous intent.

Types of Humor

Humor in the classroom can take many forms. Some of these include jokes, puns, funny facial expressions, imitating others, spontaneous comments, cartoons, videos, self-deprecating comments, wry remarks, absurd deeds, and sound effects. This variety is one of the great features of humor. It is possible for an instructor to mix and match the format of humor to both individual tastes and the tastes of the audience. Every teacher does not need to have a collection of jokes or be able to come up with a witty retort. A simple comic related to the discussion may be all that is required. Instructors should feel confident in bringing humor into their classes because, as Gordon notes, "Humor and laughter not only can coexist with rigorous learning and investigation, but can actually enhance them."[22] Specific examples of how to use humor within the library can be found in Vossler and Sheidlower, who have written a book offering techniques on how librarians can use humor within their instruction sessions.[23]

There are two main categories of humor and its application to education: humor related to the instructional content and humor unrelated to the content. While unrelated humor can be successfully utilized as an icebreaker, the most successful educational use of humor is when it is related to the content. It is this humor that helps students learn. Kaplan and Pascoe showed that when content is presented humorously, it is retained by the students over a longer period of time.[24] In this way, content humor not only provides the benefits of non-context humor but it also addresses the underlying objective of all education, which is for students to learn. This is also important in library sessions, as there is so much content to cover within a short span of time. By integrating humor into the content, it is possible to accomplish two goals at once: piquing students' interest, and connecting to the content.

Considerations in Using Humor

Humor does not need to provoke laughter to be successful. Sometimes you may just be rewarded with a smile from students who, even if they did not find the humor funny, at least recognize your attempt at adding humor to your instruction. This is one method of developing a welcoming atmosphere within the classroom. This welcoming atmosphere is also critical in order to promote laughter in the first place. The instructor must show the students that he or she is willing to laugh before expecting them to laugh. This can be helped by smiling and engaging in light chitchat before the session. This same recommendation is given whenever an instructor is trying to connect with students.

Students are not the only ones to be considered when implementing humor in the classroom. Librarians may offer the same or a similar instruction session dozens of times during the school year, as we present sessions to different sections of the same course. Delivering the same dry presentation to each class is one way to bore not only the students but ourselves. By adding humor, the instruction librarian can at the very least lighten his or her own mood with something amusing. I have also found that while students may not think I am funny, they do think it is amusing when I laugh at my own jokes.

Vulnerability

Another aspect of the use of humor is that it puts the instructor in a vulnerable position. This vulnerability stems from the fact that it is quite simple for an attempt at humor to fail. Students may not understand the instructor's humor, they may become offended, or they may simply not find it funny. Humor also creates vulnerability as the instructor's humor often gives a great deal of insight into his or her personality beyond the librarian persona. So, you are punny? Ah, you enjoy slapstick? As librarians, we often deal with students in short one-shot sessions, and it can be hard to open up at any level to a group of individuals whom we have just met.

Vulnerability, however, can also be one of the most appealing aspects of a successful teacher. This willingness to look silly or to fail is an important personalizing component in connecting with students. Especially considering that research is often an inherently messy and difficult process, it is beneficial for students to see that everyone, including the librarian, may experience difficulty. Sharing flaws with students allows them to admit to their flaws. One of the nice things about humor is that it can be used to highlight personal flaws to both show that you are human and enforce the concepts you are attempting to describe.

For example, in class I might share a story about the importance of developing keywords. I was trying to find cat-themed treats for a birthday party. In the past, I had thrown a *Minecraft* party and searched *Minecraft* treats in order to get ideas for snacks. So this time, I tried searching cat treats, but all that came back was food for cats. I needed better keywords and had to try again. This quick example shows how just typing the first thing that comes to mind is not the most successful method of getting information. It also shows that I am not without flaws, and that research can take time and thought.

Professionalism

Humor is avoided by some librarians, as they believe that it will make them appear less professional. This is a feeling that can be seen throughout higher education, stemming from the origin of higher education when learning was a serious endeavor. This perception has been perpetuated, even though the structure of education has changed dramatically within the ensuing years. It was in the mid-twentieth century that humor began to take a larger role in education, and it is now seen as increasingly acceptable throughout every level of education.

Librarians are serious about the important role they have as instructors, and thus, they work hard to gain the respect of the students. Unfortunately, this desire to be respected can result in a demeanor that pushes people away rather than bringing them in. While the instruction sessions offered by librarians provide useful information to students, it is often the case that additional learning occurs after the instruction session, when the students come to visit the librarian one-on-one. If librarians do not encourage that interaction by presenting a welcoming demeanor, they are not being as successful as they could be.

Instructor, Not Comedian

When using humor in instruction it is also important to remember that you are not a comedian performing a stand-up act. There is no expectation that you should maintain a constant stream of humorous comments, jokes, or stunts. Rather, it is better for the humor to be sparse at irregular intervals. This helps maintain the interest of the students, as they are required to pay attention in order to hear the next humorous thing. This means that you may have three examples of humor to use within one session.

If you are starting to use humor in your classroom, also remember that you are not the only possible source of humor. Students can also be a great resource for humor. By letting students know early in the class that you accept and encourage humor, you make a space where they are also allowed to make humorous contributions. This allows them to provide humorous answers to questions or examples. It is important at this point to make sure that you do not shut down the humor. Nothing kills a lighthearted mood more than a strict retort to a humorous comment. If possible, use the humorous remark provided by the student as a springboard to move forward. If it is not possible to use the comment, make sure you smile, laugh, and then ask for another response. Students are in this way able to utilize humor but also interact with the content.

To offer one simple example, I sometimes have my classes divide into groups and describe their step-by-step research process. One group started their list: *(1) Wait until the night before it is due. (2) Drink a lot of coffee to pull an all-nighter.* And from that point they went on to list the full research process including limiting their topic and evaluating their sources. The class laughed at the honesty in their process as we were able to share in a common experience, but they also fulfilled their task of developing a research process. I shared in their laughter and noted how they had a lot of time in their all-nighter in order to complete the in-depth research they described next. This group's process also allowed me to interject the fact that it takes time to do research, so it is always better to start sooner. In this way, the humor the students provided was the impetus for more learning than may have otherwise occurred.

Appropriate Humor

Humor should always be used toward the achievement of an educational goal. Like all pedagogical approaches, humor should be applied conscientiously. Any new teaching technique requires an investment of time and energy, so be aware that it will be important to work on developing your approach to humor and continuing to assess and revise its effectiveness. It takes time to successfully implement humor, so it is important to dedicate yourself to the idea.

There are four appropriate types of humor noted by Wanzer and colleagues: topic-related humor, humor unrelated to a topic, self-disparaging humor, and unplanned humor.[25] **Topic-related humor** is often the best use of humor in the classroom. It is often the humorous example of a concept that sticks with the students and helps promote their learning. Garner notes that for humor to be successful, it must be "specific, targeted, and appropriate to the subject matter."[26] As noted earlier, **humor that is unrelated to the topic** is often best used as an icebreaker or as a way to set the tone of the session. Showing a humorous comic or GIF as the students enter the classroom can help grab their attention, while a random joke in the middle of the session can cause confusion.

Self-deprecating humor is often discussed as a good form of humor to be used in the classroom context. This can be one way to avoid any humor that reflects negativity onto the students. Self-deprecating humor also focuses attention on the instructor, thereby humanizing him or her as a librarian. One class session with students is not much time to allow them to get to know and trust you. Self-deprecating humor can be a way to share personal information with the students; it can also show that you are willing to fail. This acknowledgement of ignorance or vulnerability lets the students know that it is also okay for them to share their confusion and questions as well.

Unplanned humor can take on any number of forms in the classroom: a witty retort to a question, an unplanned result coming up during a search, or a technical failure taken in stride. Humor can also be used to lessen the impact of a criticism. In this way, humor can be an effective way to bring students back to task when they are not paying attention or if they are doing something inappropriate in the classroom.

Inappropriate Humor

While it may seem obvious, humor should never be used to ridicule someone or denigrate a group of individuals. This is a quick way to turn an apathetic group of students into a hostile group of students. While students understand sarcasm and may find it humorous in other situations, when it is directed at them or one of their classmates they will close up and withdraw from the instruction. Humor used in this way causes fear. It is also best to avoid profanity, vulgarity, and sexual innuendo when selecting humor to use in the classroom.

Humor may be "highly personal, subjective, and contextual."[27] Especially as classrooms become increasingly diverse, it is important to consider the various cultures and backgrounds of the students. This cultural awareness relates to a number of issues experienced by students. Humor should not be offensive to anyone; thus cultural differences should never be used as a way to isolate and ridicule a group. The instructor should consider also that different cultures have varying traditions and codes of conduct. A joke about eating meat may not be funny to a student with religious dietary restrictions, just as a joke making fun of bosses may not go over well with someone from a strict authoritarian background. Understanding these differences, knowing your students, and celebrating diversity rather than denigrating it will result in a more productive classroom.

Cultural humor also comes into play when one considers that often, for humor to be successful, all individuals must have a related understanding of the topic. Often this occurs within groups that have grown up in the same area and experienced similar upbringings. A shared set of experiences results in a deeper understanding of why something may be funny. Thus, it is possible to share with a class of students from the United States stories about high school sports or prom or Saturday morning cartoons. These are experiences that they know and can relate to. However, for some international students, humorous comments on these and other culture-specific topics can result in their feeling excluded from the group.

The importance of individuals having a connection also comes into play with many pop culture references. As popular songs, movies, and television shows continue to evolve, a reference that may have had students laughing a year ago may now provoke a sad smile and will soon result in a confused stare. When using pop culture as a source of humor, it is never good to force the reference. If you legitimately like the song, movie, or show, feel free to use it. Your passion and excitement will show through. However, if you try to reference something with no knowledge of the topic, the students will see that. In such instances, they may see an adult trying to fit in and be cool. This view distracts from the open, friendly professional image you are trying to project.

Intrinsic Motivational Factors

As noted in chapter 1, there are seven factors that promote intrinsic motivation. Humor addresses the following factors:

- **Fantasy**—Humor often contains a high amount of fantasy. Many jokes put the listener into a situation beyond the norm. Comics do something similar by having viewers consider a world beyond their own.

- **Curiosity**—The success of humor often relies on the curiosity of the intended individuals, in that the setup will cause a questioning of their knowledge that is resolved by the punchline.

Conclusion

Implementing humor in the classroom can be a slightly risky undertaking. However, given the number of possible benefits, it is something that should be consciously added to an instructional session. A failed joke or attempt at humor may seem critical to the presenter, but remember that for the students this is not a serious situation. At the very worst they may remember the librarian tried to be funny and really was not. More likely they will think: the librarian tried to make the session fun; that was nice of them; I think I will go ask them a question.

Finally, humor should not be seen as the cure-all for instruction. Adding one joke or humorous cultural reference into your instruction session will not magically impart to students the knowledge they need to be information-literate. However, a small amount of humor may motivate them to connect with the instructional content a little more deeply and thus be prepared to move further along toward the goal of feeling comfortable working with information.

Notes

1. Cris Mayo, "Being in on the Joke: Pedagogy, Race, Humor," *Philosophy of Education Yearbook 2008*: 245.

2. Kanwar Saurabh Singh, Adarsh Tripathi, and Ajay Kohli, "Humour in Psychiatric Clinical Practice," *Delhi Psychiatry Journal* 14, no. 2 (2011): 232–36.

3. Rod A. Martin, "Humor, Laughter, and Physical Health: Methodological Issues and Research Findings," *Psychological Bulletin* 127, no. 4 (2001): 504–19; Paul E. McGhee, "Comprehensive Review of Humor Research" (paper presented at the annual meeting of the Association for Applied and Therapeutic Humor, Baltimore, MD, February 2002); Robert R. Provine, *Laughter* (New York: Viking Penguin, 2000).

4. Linda Meyer Englert, "Learning with Laughter: Using Humor in the Nursing Classroom," *Nursing Education Perspectives* 31, no. 1 (2010): 48–49; Julia Wilkins and Amy Janel Eisenbraun, "Humor Theories and the Physiological Benefits of Laughter," *Holistic Nursing Practice* 23, no. 6 (2009): 349–54.
5. Ronald Berk and Joy P. Nanda, "Effects of Jocular Instructional Methods on Attitudes, Anxiety, and Achievement in Statistics Courses," *HUMOR: International Journal of Humor Research* 11, no. 4 (1998): 383–409.
6. Ronald Berk, *Humor as an Instructional Defibrillator* (Sterling, VA: Stylus Publishing, 2002).
7. Ibid.
8. Debra Korobkin, "Humor in the Classroom," *College Teaching* 36, no. 4 (1988): 154–58.
9. Joshua Vossler and Scott Sheidlower, *Humor and Information Literacy* (Santa Barbara, CA: Libraries Unlimited, 2011).
10. Berk, *Humor as an Instructional Defibrillator*.
11. Korobkin, "Humor in the Classroom"; Deborah Hill, *Humor in the Classroom* (Springfield, IL: C. C. Thomas, 1988); R. L. Garner, "Humor in Pedagogy: How Ha-Ha Can Lead to Aha!" *College Teaching* 54, no. 1 (2006): 177–80; Melissa Bekelja Wanzer and Ann Bainbridge Frymier, "The Relationship between Student Perceptions of Instructor Humor and Student's Reports of Learning," *Communication Education* 48, no. 1 (1999): 48–62; G. Haigh, "Do Smile: But Don't Tell Too Many Jokes," *Times (London) Educational Supplement,* January 8, 1999: 13B; Elizabeth N. Millard, "Humor Can Be a Serious Strategy," *Delta Kappa Gamma Bulletin* 65, no. 3 (1999): 9–14; Avner Ziv, "Facilitating Effects of Humor on Creativity," *Journal of Education Psychology* 68, no. 3 (1976): 318–22; Colleen Ruggieri, "Laugh and Learn: Using Humor to Teach Tragedy," *English Journal* 88, no. 4 (1999): 53–58; David Lazear, *Seven Ways of Knowing* (Palatine, IL: Skylight Publishing, 1991).
12. Neelam Kher, Susan Molstad, and Roberta Donahue, "Using Humor in the College Classroom to Enhance Teaching Effectiveness in 'Dread Courses,'" *College Student Journal* 33, no. 3 (1999): 400–6.
13. Gayle Webb White, "Teachers' Report of How They Used Humor with Students Perceived Use of Such Humor," *Education* 122, no. 2 (2001): 337–47.
14. Garner, "Humor in Pedagogy," 177.
15. John A. Banas, Norah Dunbar, Dariela Rodriguez, and Shr-Jie Liu, "A Review of Humor in Educational Settings: Four Decades of Research," *Communication Education* 60, no. 1 (2011): 137.
16. Berk and Nanda, "Effects of Jocular Instructional Methods."
17. Billie E. Walker, "Using Humor in Library Instruction," *Reference Services Review* 34, no. 1 (2006): 125.
18. David James, "A Need for Humor in Online Courses," *College Teaching* 52, no. 3 (2004): 93–94.
19. Jehad Imlawi and Dawn Gregg, "Engagement in Online Social Networks: The Impact of Self-Disclosure and Humor," *International Journal of Human-Computer Interaction* 30, no. 2 (2014): 106–25.
20. Franziska J. Köbler and Marco M. Nitzschner, "The Efficiency of Different Online Learning Media: An Empirical Study," in *11th International Conference: Cognition and Exploratory Learning in the Digital Age, 2014: Proceedings,* ed. Demetrios G. Sampson, J. Michael Spector, Dirk Ifenthaler, and Pedro Isaias (IADIS Press, 2014), 244–48.

21. Ugur Basarmak and Ahmet Mahiroglu, "The Effect of Online Learning Environment Based on Caricature Animation Used in Science and Technology Course on the Success and Attitude of the Student for Humor," *Turkish Online Journal of Educational Technology—TOJET* 15, no. 4 (2016): 107–18.
22. Mordechai Gordon, "Learning to Laugh at Ourselves: Humor, Self-Transcendence, and the Cultivation of Moral Virtues," *Educational Theory* 60, no. 6 (2011): 749.
23. Vossler and Sheidlower, *Humor and Information Literacy.*
24. Robert M. Kaplan and Gregory C. Pascoe, "Humorous Lectures and Humorous Examples: Some Effects upon Comprehension and Retention," *College Student Journal* 33, no. 3 (1977): 400–7.
25. Melissa Bekelja Wanzer, Ann Bainbridge Frymier, Ann M. Wojtaszczyk, and Tony Smith, "Appropriate and Inappropriate Uses of Humor by Teachers," *Communication Education* 55, no. 2 (2006): 178–96.
26. Garner, "Humor in Pedagogy," 178.
27. Ibid.

Bibliography

Banas, John A., Norah Dunbar, Dariela Rodriguez, and Shr-Jie Liu. "A Review of Humor in Educational Settings: Four Decades of Research." *Communication Education* 60, no. 1 (2011): 115–44.

Basarmak, Ugur, and Ahmet Mahiroglu. "The Effect of Online Learning Environment Based on Caricature Animation Used in Science and Technology Course on the Success and Attitude of the Student for Humor." *Turkish Online Journal of Educational Technology—TOJET* 15, no. 4 (2016): 107–18.

Berk, Ronald. *Humor as an Instructional Defibrillator.* Sterling, VA: Stylus Publishing, 2002.

Berk, Ronald, and Joy P. Nanda. "Effects of Jocular Instructional Methods on Attitudes, Anxiety, and Achievement in Statistics Courses." *HUMOR: International Journal of Humor Research* 11, no. 4 (1998): 383–409.

Englert, Linda Meyer. "Learning with Laughter: Using Humor in the Nursing Classroom." *Nursing Education Perspectives* 31, no. 1 (2010): 48–49.

Garner, R. L. "Humor in Pedagogy: How Ha-Ha Can Lead to Aha!" *College Teaching* 54, no. 1 (2006): 177–80.

Gordon, Mordechai. "Learning to Laugh at Ourselves: Humor, Self-Transcendence, and the Cultivation of Moral Virtues." *Educational Theory* 60, no. 6 (2011): 735–49.

Haigh, G. "Do Smile: But Don't Tell Too Many Jokes." *Times (London) Educational Supplement,* January 8, 1999: 13B.

Hill, Deborah. *Humor in the Classroom: A Handbook for Teachers (and Other Entertainers).* Springfield, IL: C. C. Thomas, 1988.

Imlawi, Jehad, and Dawn Gregg. "Engagement in Online Social Networks: The Impact of Self-Disclosure and Humor." *International Journal of Human-Computer Interaction* 30, no. 2 (2014): 106–25.

James, David. "A Need for Humor in Online Courses." *College Teaching* 52, no. 3 (2004): 93–94.

Kaplan, Robert M., and Gregory C. Pascoe. "Humorous Lectures and Humorous Examples: Some Effects upon Comprehension and Retention." *College Student Journal* 33, no. 3 (1977): 400–7.

Kher, Neelam, Susan Molstad, and Roberta Donahue. "Using Humor in the College Classroom to Enhance Teaching Effectiveness in 'Dread Courses.'" *College Student Journal* 33, no. 3 (1999): 400–6.

Köbler, Franziska J., and Marco M. Nitzschner. "The Efficiency of Different Online Learning Media: An Empirical Study." In *11th International Conference: Cognition and Exploratory Learning in the Digital Age, 2014: Proceedings.* Edited by Demetrios G. Sampson, J. Michael Spector, Dirk Ifenthaler, and Pedro Isaias, 244–48. IADIS Press, 2014.

Korobkin, Debra. "Humor in the Classroom." *College Teaching* 36, no. 4 (1988): 154–58.

Lazear, David. *Seven Ways of Knowing.* Palatine, IL: Skylight Publishing, 1991.

Martin, Rod A. "Humor, Laughter, and Physical Health: Methodological Issues and Research Findings." *Psychological Bulletin* 127, no. 4 (2001): 504–19.

Mayo, Cris. "Being in on the Joke: Pedagogy, Race, Humor." *Philosophy of Education Yearbook 2008*: 244–52.

McGhee, Paul E. "Comprehensive Review of Humor Research." Paper presented at the annual meeting of the Association for Applied and Therapeutic Humor, Baltimore, MD, February 2002.

Millard, Elizabeth N. "Humor Can Be a Serious Strategy." *Delta Kappa Gamma Bulletin* 65, no. 3 (1999): 9–14.

Provine, Robert R. *Laughter: A Scientific Investigation.* New York: Viking Penguin, 2000.

Ruggieri, Colleen. "Laugh and Learn: Using Humor to Teach Tragedy." *English Journal* 88, no. 4 (1999): 53–58.

Singh, Kanwar Saurabh, Adarsh Tripathi, and Ajay Kohli. "Humour in Psychiatric Clinical Practice." *Delhi Psychiatry Journal* 14, no. 2 (2011): 232–36.

Vossler, Joshua, and Scott Sheidlower. *Humor and Information Literacy: Practical Techniques for Library Instruction.* Santa Barbara, CA: Libraries Unlimited, 2011.

Walker, Billie E. "Using Humor in Library Instruction." *Reference Services Review* 34, no. 1 (2006): 117–28.

Wanzer, Melissa Bekelja, and Ann Bainbridge Frymier. "The Relationship between Student Perceptions of Instructor Humor and Student's Reports of Learning." *Communication Education* 48, no. 1 (1999): 48–62.

Wanzer, Melissa Bekelja, Ann Bainbridge Frymier, Ann M. Wojtaszczyk, and Tony Smith. "Appropriate and Inappropriate Uses of Humor by Teachers." *Communication Education* 55, no. 2 (2006): 178–96.

White, Gayle Webb. "Teachers' Report of How They Used Humor with Students Perceived Use of Such Humor." *Education* 122, no. 2 (2001): 337–47.

Wilkins, Julia, and Amy Janel Eisenbraun. "Humor Theories and the Physiological Benefits of Laughter." *Holistic Nursing Practice* 23, no. 6 (2009): 349–54.

Ziv, Avner. "Facilitating Effects of Humor on Creativity." *Journal of Education Psychology* 68, no. 3 (1976): 318–22.

CHAPTER 4

Games

For when the One Great Scorer comes to mark against your name,

He writes—not that you won or lost—but how you played the Game.[1]

There is a great variety of games in all mediums: board games, card games, video games, computer games, strategy games, sport games, role-playing games, and on and on. While not everyone may enjoy every game, there is surely a game for everyone. People commonly note they are "playing a game," but while play and games are often connected and discussed together, there is an important difference between the two in this book. Play relates to fun and enjoyment within an unstructured setting. Within this book, *games* will refer to a structured experience in which **one or more individuals compete under a common set of rules and guidelines in order to achieve a goal**. An important component that is not included in that definition, but is true of games presented later in this book, is the fact that mental effort is required to succeed in reaching the goal of these games. Thus, those games that rely solely on luck, such as the board game *Candyland* or the card game *War*, will not be presented.

Games and game-play elements are seen fairly regularly in the context of elementary school classrooms, but as students age, teachers often incorporate fewer and fewer games into their classroom instruction. Perhaps they think that it is time to put away childish things, but "they need to understand that the game interface is just the motivational engine that encourages students to delve deeply into the system, encouraging them to develop skills and knowledge."[2]

Gamification and Game-Based Learning

Gamification and *game-based learning* are terms that are widely used in discussions and literature surrounding the use of games in education. Since they both refer to games, many think that they mean the same thing. However, just as not all gamers are equal, neither are these two terms. There is a major difference between gamification and game-based learning, and as a result, how and when they are applied in the classroom will vary.

Gamification

Gamification (the verb form is **to gamify**) is the application of game design thinking and mechanics to non-game applications in order to enhance motivation, engagement, and fun. The game design elements that are frequently applied to an educational setting are

- **Challenges**—These are the tasks that the players are expected to complete. Within a classroom, example challenges may include watching a video, completing an assignment, reading a chapter, or working on a project.

- **Points**—Sometimes known as experience points (XP), points are often accumulated in order to level up. Points are earned by completing tasks within the game or lessons within the classroom. Points can be used to compare players to each other on a leaderboard.

- **Currency**—Virtual currency is earned by completing tasks or levels within the game. One possible use of currency might be to purchase rewards or upgrades. Within a classroom, possible rewards could possibly be extra points on a test or help with a question.

- **Leveling up**—This is a way to encourage participants to continue progress through the game. As new levels are reached, a variety of prizes, opportunities, or rewards can be unlocked.

- **Leaderboards**—Interject competition into the game by ranking the participants according to the number of points they have earned. Within a classroom, this can encourage students to complete more challenges or tasks. This can include additional projects that may be considered extra credit in another classroom.

- **Badges**—Participants earn badges by completing a task or earning a set number of points. Within the classroom, these badges can be either physical items such as stickers or virtual image representations.

While these game design elements are used as the building blocks of applying gamification to an educational setting, it is also important to consider how these blocks are put together. Just because the pieces are all there does not automatically mean that the game will be a success and students will automatically engage with the content and learn. There are additional considerations that must be applied when gamifying the classroom.

- The game must have a clear **goal and rules**. As in any game, it is important for the players to know what they are attempting to do and how they need to accomplish it. Since gamification of the classroom may be different than anything else that the students have experienced, it is especially critical that the students understand what is expected of them.

- **Challenges** should be challenging but achievable. This is the same principle that should be applied to all lesson plans and assignments in the classroom. Students should be pushed to learn something new but not so overwhelmed by the content that they shut down and avoid the material. The gamification process can be aided in this by providing review or basic challenges for those who need them. Completing these challenges will result in the earning of a few points or some similar reward. This allows those who need to review the content the opportunity to still feel as if they are progressing, while those who do not need the content review can move forward with the main challenge for more points.

- **Feedback** is also very important within a game. Within many games, especially video games, players know almost immediately whether their action has resulted in a positive or negative outcome. This feedback drives future actions, and the players learn how to successfully maneuver within the game. Prompt feedback is also critical in the classroom. When students complete a challenge, they want to know as soon as possible what they have earned in points, currency, or badges, and how that changes their level or place on the leaderboard. It is up to the instructors to do what they can to provide accelerated feedback. This is also similar to a traditional classroom in which feedback from the instructor is often considered one of the basic characteristics of an effective teacher.

- One of the appealing features of games is the fact that it is always possible to **start over**. Losing or failing is not the end. Often, the player takes what has been learned about the game and begins again. This is not only accepted but expected within a game. Games that are so simple that they can be mastered in the first attempt are often not satisfying to players. There is more satisfaction in being able to improve and overcome obstacles in repeated attempts. This is an important aspect of games that can be applied to education. Getting a question wrong or a poor grade should not be the end. It should be up to the students to learn why they were wrong and apply that knowledge to the next task in order to prove that they have mastered the concept. This reiterative process of continuing to work until a concept is learned is an important component of game play. It means that students will continue to work through a problem if it means they will earn points and continue to level up.

- Another characteristic from the field of education that can be applied in gamification is encouraging students to take an active part in their education by giving them **control** or say over aspects of the game. For example, students may determine the rewards in the game. This insures that the rewards are items that they would appreciate and consider worth the work required. This enhances a connection and commitment toward completing the challenges. Another way to give control to students is to let them choose how they want to meet a challenge. For example, if the challenge is showing an understanding of Boolean operators, the students could write an essay, make a video, give a presentation, create a meme, and so on. The important thing is for them to have an element of control.

Gamification has been applied both within individual classrooms and by online groups and companies that provide their courses to users. One of the best-known of these companies is Khan Academy. Khan Academy is run by a nonprofit group offering personalized instruction in math, science, computer programming, history, art history, economics, and more. The lessons are offered for free and have been translated into forty languages. Teachers or parents can create accounts for their students to go through the lessons and earn points.

Gamification requires an immersive environment in order for students to make a connection with the game aspect of education. It will take time for them to go through the various challenges in order to earn points, currency, and badges and advance through levels in order to rise on the leaderboard. Due to this, gamification works best when the game will continue over a long period of time. It is also critical to clearly think through the application of gamification and be very deliberate in the development of challenges. If done poorly, gamification can fail to engage students or result in students not learning the content.

Game-Based Learning

Game-based learning is the integration of a game into education to facilitate learning. Games used in this manner do not drive the entire learning experience. They are used instead as short components within the classroom as a means of offering variety in the instruction offered. These games can either be digital or analog. They often involve an element of competition, either as students play against each other or as they try to beat their own personal scores. Many games will also contain an element of fantasy, often involving a storyline through which the student must progress to reach the learning outcome.

When using game-based learning, it is important that that learning outcomes be connected to the earning of points and success within the game. Some games that purport to be educational compartmentalize the education content from the game content, with the students going through a cycle of learning something, doing something fun, learning something, doing something fun, and so on. This format does not work to engage the students with the educational content, as they can begin to see the learning aspect as a negative component that they must get through in order to reach the fun. A true educational game makes learning the fun aspect.

Game-based learning does not require the complete immersive environment seen in gamification, and thus it can be used during brief sessions with students. It is still important that the games chosen be utilized for a specific purpose and enhance the learning process. A greater variety of game genres and formats can also be integrated into game-based learning in order to connect with students.

Benefits of Games

When you ask someone to play a game, depending on that individual's background, he or she may picture of range of different situations: a family sitting around a board game, adults playing bridge with a deck of cards, teenagers on a couch playing video games, kids running around playing soccer, or a pair of friends sitting across from each other with a set of *Magic* cards. While each of these scenarios requires different skills, there is one thing they all have in common: the game is social. Social interaction and the development of social skills is one of the first benefits of games. Games allow for individuals to interact with others, providing a social connection that is critical for all humans. Games also allow for individuals to develop social skills such as communication, sharing, compromising, taking turns, appropriate competition, and collaboration.

In addition to these social skills, games also promote higher-level thinking skills.[3] Various games can address a range of skills including recall of information, long-term planning, strategic analysis, synthesis of information, inquiry, problem solving, critical thinking, creativity, and systems thinking.

While all games offer these benefits to varying degrees, there are also studies that look specifically at the benefits of frequent playing of recreational video games. These benefits include enhanced inductive reasoning, metacognition, memory, spatial visualization and mental rotation, and spatial distribution of attention and visual selective attention.[4]

Physical benefits have also been seen in the use of *exergames*, games which incorporate exercise and therefore require more energy expenditure than sedentary games. Game players have shown an increase in the skills of task switching and perceptual speed.[5]

Research Studies of Games in the Classroom

Games are often the first iteration of learning that children are exposed to. As Hwang and Wu note, "Games are an important part of the development of children's cognition and social processes."[6] One of the benefits of games is the fact that they are flexible; they can be used in the classroom at various times within a unit in order to achieve a range of purposes. They can be used to introduce a new topic by providing a unique experience to gain the attention of the students. They can be used throughout a unit in order to help the students apply what they have already learned. This allows for a deeper connection with the content by allowing the students to interact with the material in a variety of methods and mediums. They can also be used at the end of a unit as a way for students to review and show their mastery of the content.

One important aspect of games is that they provide a safe place in which to learn and work through given content. As noted by Kim, games "offer an environment intentionally designed to provide people with optimal experience by means of various gaming mechanisms and dynamics."[7] Games can also be developed with the option of being played by individuals or by teams. This is discussed by Yaman and Covington, who note that effective games are developed to combine the dynamics of group cooperation with competition in the game itself.[8]

Guillen-Nieto and Aleson-Carbonell list three pedagogical changes that have affected the implementation of games in the classroom: (1) a shift from teacher-centered to learner-centered education; (2) a shift from learning by listening to learning by doing; and (3) a shift from memory of a concept to the capacity to find and use information.[9] Drawing on these changes, it can be asserted that games are useful educational tools by virtue of their interactivity. As Aldrich notes, the interactivity of games requires that the "learning goals are not just the traditional 'learning to know' type, but also 'learning to be' and 'learning to do.'"[10]

Research on the use of games in education shows they provide motivating learning experiences,[11] they help students to engage with course work,[12] and they improve desired learning outcomes.[13] Huizenga and colleagues note that the "learning potential of mobile and location-based technologies [such as games] lies in the possibility to embed learning in an authentic environment, enhance engagement and foster learning outside traditional formal educational settings."[14]

Instructional Benefits

"Although some educators question the value of games, they need to understand that the game interface is just the 'motivational engine' that encourages students to delve deeply into the system, encouraging them to develop skills and knowledge."[15] There are a number of characteristics of games that make them beneficial when applied in the classroom context. First, games are familiar to students. If you tell them, "We are going to play a game in class," it ignites their interest, as they have past experiences with games and know that they should provide fun and enjoyment. Games can also be easy to explain, given the fact that the students may already have experience with a similar game. If you say, "This game is like *Jeopardy*," the students will already have an understanding of many of the rules and purpose of the game. Because of their familiar aspects, games are also very approachable for students.

Games can also be integrated into the classroom for various lengths of time. Gamification of the classroom requires the game to continue throughout the entire length of the class. But it is also possible to play a game within a ten-minute period. This ability to insert games into a class session is beneficial, as it is helpful to have students participate in a range of activities within class in order to maintain motivation and promote their engagement.

Games are also nonthreatening, in that students know that within games, failure or losing is always possible but carries no penalty. In fact, even when something bad happens in a game, there is another chance for success. Risk taking is also accepted as a component of games. Compare this to some classrooms where students may fear to give an answer or ask a question. Promoting the idea that a risk can result in a positive result is helpful, as students can apply this understanding to their other interactions outside of the game where life is not always as safe as they might hope.

Games are also the epitome of interaction. If students are playing a game, they must engage at some level. This active learning is an important benefit of games, as learning cannot occur if the students do not interact with the content in some way. This interaction is also important, in that games can be used as a way to have students connect to content that may be considered otherwise boring. By initiating interest and excitement for a topic, games also create experiences for the students that may be more memorable. This can encourage later recall of the content.

This interaction also extends to other classmates. Collaborative learning can be a powerful tool, and by playing games together students have shared experiences that promote community development. Students also are able to share their insights and understanding during the game-playing process, allowing them to learn from one another.

Games and Technology

One major focus of the research on the benefits of games centers on digital games. As millennials and the following generation continue to move through the education system, we find students who are more and more comfortable within a digital environment. Desktop computers are being replaced by mobile interfaces, and with each new advancement in technology, education has incorporated those technologies into the classroom to both meet students where they live and to help prepare them to work with these technologies in the future.

As games were first developed for the digital medium, they were known as *edutainment*. This encompassed a variety of software programs that were developed to both educate and entertain. Recently, this term has been replaced by the term *serious games*. Interest in serious games continues as the number of individuals who play games either regularly or casually continues to rise. eMarketer shows increases in both tablet and console gaming.[16] A little over 40 percent of video and computer gamers are female, as seen in surveys by the Entertainment Software Association from 2006 to 2016.[17] So games continue to reach an increasing number of both males and females.

Simulations and virtual worlds can also fall under the classification of digital games. Simulations put students into a safe environment where they can respond to real-life situations without the fear of failure. Some of the better-known educational simulations include those in the medical field and flight simulations. Virtual worlds allow students to take on a role within the game that gives them the power to make decisions concerning how that world will run. The various *SimCity* games would be the best-known of this genre, as players decide how to run a city, manage a farm, or develop amusement parks.

Serious games require students to process new content and then apply it. This is especially important as education is not meant to be solely focused on a student's ability to repeat a concept but rather the ability to transfer knowledge in order to apply the concept to a variety of situations. "The promise of the instructional technology is that educational games can improve students' engagement with their own learning in a way that increases students' proficiency as well as their willingness to attempt frustrating but potentially rewarding experiences in academic subjects that otherwise might not be appealing."[18]

Gee provides a list of learning principles that are found within video games: cycles of challenges and challenges just beyond the player's comfort level, situated meaning, low consequences for failure, and just-in-time information.[19] Mayo also provides a list of elements that promote the use of serious games: massive reach, experiential learning, enquiry-based learning, self-efficacy, goal setting, cooperation, continuous feedback, enhanced brain chemistry, and time on task.[20] The Federation of American Scientists' *Summit on Educational Games* identified a list of educational strategies that are present in video games.

- clear learning goals
- practice opportunities
- monitoring of progress, provision of continual feedback
- moving of player to higher challenges
- encouraging of inquiry and questions
- contextual bridging

- time on task
- motivation
- scaffolding
- personalization
- infinitely patient medium[21]

There is also evidence that digital games promote neural plasticity and cognitive abilities. These are traits that are also used when learning.[22] This finding would explain why frequent gamers continue to develop more advanced skill and strategy within their gameplay.

Types of Games

Games come in a variety of forms, from *Jeopardy*-like quizzes to virtual world computer simulations. When integrating a game into the classroom, there are two main types that can be used. First are games that were developed specifically to be used for education. Within libraries, a well-known example is *TILT*, the Texas Information Literacy Tutorial. The second variety is games that are created for the general public that instructors have adapted for classroom use. These are referred to as commercial, off-the-shelf (COTS). Some examples include *Civilization* and *1960: The Making of the President*.

Within these two larger types of games, there is another categorization between digital games (within this book, anything that relies on computers or other game consoles to deliver the games) and analog games (within this book, a game that does not require technology.)

Considerations

It should be noted that there is the risk when using games in education that the focus is shifted too much toward the game and away from the desired learning outcomes. As Guillen-Nieto and Aleson-Carbonell assert, "A key challenge for designers then is to get the correct balance between delightful play and fulfilling specified learning outcomes."[23] This point is also emphasized by Yaman and Covington, who argue that "the focus should be on what was learned, not who won the game."[24]

Care should also be taken when implementing game elements in either an individual game or an entire class. The game elements are critical, as they are what work together to create a rich, engaging experience for the students to learn, but if implemented poorly they can have negative impacts. Aldrich offers some of the potential negative results of poor implementation of game elements:

- They take time to develop, which can take away from the development of the actual learning content.
- They are experienced by different players in different ways, meaning while some may enjoy them, others may dislike them.
- Competition may shift the focus for students from learning to getting the high score.
- Poorly implemented game elements can be seen as lame by students.
- Too few game elements result in dry games, while too many can result in an overwhelming, silly game.[25]

When implementing games in the classroom, the instructor must first decide whether to use a pre-existing game or to develop a new game. There are benefits and drawbacks to each approach. For a pre-existing game it is not necessary to take time to develop the game, but it will take time to discover an appropriate game to use, and the content may not address the specific learning objectives, requiring possible adjustments. By developing a new game tailored to specific content, the instructor has the opportunity to individualize the content to meet specific learning objectives in relation to unique organizational characteristics. However, it does take time and experience to create a game.

Not all games are created equal in relation to the type of learning that they promote. While it is possible to promote deep learning through the use of certain games, these games often require a time commitment that is not available during one class period. This deep learning will require multiple interactions with the game in order to make mistakes and gain insight. This does not mean, however, that games do not have a place within library instruction. The learning outcomes of short games will focus more on introduction to a topic or review of concepts. These goals are no less important, and the engaging motivation provided by games makes them a powerful instructional technique to apply to a library session.

Intrinsic Motivational Factors

As noted in chapter 1, there are seven factors that promote intrinsic motivation. Games address the following factors.

- **Challenge**—The central tenet of games is that the players must try to reach a goal. This goal is met by overcoming a range of challenges.

- **Fantasy**—Games often put players into situations beyond their normal world. These games also allow them to experience fantasy as they earn money or power or success within the game.

- **Recognition**—Success within a game results in recognition from other players, either by being declared the winner or by being added to a leaderboard.

- **Control**—Games allow players to make their own choices on actions and events. This control over what is done gives players a feeling of ownership of their fate.

- **Competition**—Games allow individuals to play against others to in order to reach the final goal. This challenge may encourage some to work harder.

Conclusion

The sample lesson plans in the second part of this book will apply game-based learning rather than gamification, as its structure is better suited to the traditional single instructional session offered by librarians. For those able to create a situation where gamification would be applicable, there are a range of books and professional webinars that address the process of gamifying the classroom.

Games can be a powerful means for librarians to connect with students in library instruction sessions. As Kim notes, "Game dynamics can raise library users' level of engagement with library resources, programs, and services," and furthermore, "They can help library users to solve problems more effectively and quickly by making the process fun."[26] As an example, Leach and Sugarman describe their use of a *Jeopardy*-like game to reinforce the content learned during their one-shot instruction sessions, and they note that "the instruction librarian should select, adapt and direct the game so that it is enjoyable for the students but also has a definite purpose and defined learning outcomes."[27]

The idea and enjoyment of games is an international commonality. It makes sense to use that human connection with games as leverage to enhance the instruction offered to students. Klopfer and colleagues offer a nice, concise summary promoting the use of games in the classroom: "Not only is this highly motivating and engaging for students, it allows students to retain, connect and transfer learning from these experiences to future learning and experiences."[28]

Notes

1. "Grantland Rice (1880–1954)." In *The Hutchinson Unabridged Encyclopedia with Atlas and Weather Guide*, edited by Helicon. (Helicon, 2016.)

2. Joan K. Lippincott, "Learning, Engagement, and Technology," chapter 9 in *Student Engagement and Information Literacy*, ed. Craig Gibson (Chicago: Association of College and Research Libraries, 2006), 174.

3. Lakshmi Prayaga and John W. Coffey, "Computer Game Development: An Instructional Strategy to Promote Higher Order Thinking Skills," *Journal of Educational Technology* 5, no. 3 (2008): 40–48; John Rice, "Assessing Higher Order Thinking in Video Games," *Journal of Technology and Teacher Education* 15, no. 1 (2007): 87–100; Zahed Siddique, Chen Ling, Piyamas Roberson, Yunjun Xu, and Xiaojun Geng, "Facilitating Higher-Order Learning through Computer Games," *Journal of Mechanical Design* 135, no. 12 (2013): 121004–10.

4. Patricia M. Greenfield, Luigia Camaioni, Paola Ercolani, Laura Weiss, Bennett A. Lauber, and Paola Perucchini, "Cognitive Socialization by Computer Games in Two Cultures: Inductive Discovery or Mastery of an Iconic Code?" *Journal of Applied Developmental Psychology* 15, no. 1 (1994): 59–85; Hitendra Pillay, "An Investigation of the Cognitive Process Engaged in by Recreational Computer Game Players: Implications for Skills of the Future," *Journal of Research on Technology in Education* 34, no. 3 (2002): 336–50; Stephanie S. VanDeventer and James A. White, "Expert Behavior in Children's Video Game Play," *Simulation and Gaming* 33, no. 1 (2002): 28–48; Walter R. Boot, Arthur F. Kramer, Daniel J. Simons, Monica Fabiana, and Gabriele Gratton, "The Effects of Video Game Playing on Attention, Memory, and Executive Control," *Acta Psychologica* 129 (2008): 387–98; Lynn Okagaki and Peter Frensch, "Effects of Video Game Playing on Measures of Spatial Performance: Gender Effects in Late Adolescence," *Journal of Applied Developmental Psychology* 15, no. 1 (1994): 33–58; C. Shawn Green and Daphne Bavelier, "Action Video Game Experience Alters the Spatial Resolution of Attention," *Psychological Science* 18, no. 1 (2007): 88–94; James W. Karle, Scott Watter, and Judith M. Shedden, "Task Switching in Video Game Players: Benefits of Selective Attention but Not Resistance to Proactive Interference," *Acta Psychologica* 134, no. 1 (2010): 70–78.

5. Amanda E. Staiano, Anisha A. Abraham, and Sandra L. Calvert, "Competitive versus Cooperative Exergame Play for African American Adolescents' Executive Function Skills: Short-Term Effects in a Long-Term Training Intervention," *Developmental Psychology* 48, no. 2 (2012): 337–42.

6. Gwo-Jen Hwang and Po-Han Wu, "Advancements and Trends in Digital Game-Based Learning Research: A Review of Publications in Selected Journals from 2001 to 2010," *British Journal of Educational Technology* 43, no. 1 (2012): E6.

7. Bohyun Kim, "Harnessing the Power of Game Dynamics," *College and Research Libraries News* 73, no. 8 (2012): 465.

8. Dan Yaman and Missy Covington, *I'll Take Learning for 500* (San Francisco: Pfeiffer, 2006), xviii.

9. Victoria Guillen-Nieto and Marian Aleson-Carbonell, "Serious Games and Learning Effectiveness: The Case of It's a Deal!" *Computers and Education* 58, no. 1 (2012): 435–48.

10. Clark Aldrich, *Learning Online with Games, Simulation, and Virtual Worlds* (San Francisco: Jossey-Bass, 2009), 15.

11. Gerhard Schwabe and Christoph Goth, "Mobile Learning with a Mobile Game: Design and Motivational Effects," *Journal of Computer Assisted Learning* 21, no. 3 (2005): 204–16; Juan C. Burguillo, "Using Game Theory and Competition-Based Learning to Stimulate Student Motivation and Performance," *Computers and Education* 55, no. 2 (2010): 566–75; Michele D. Dickey, "Murder on Grimm Isle: The Impact of Game Narrative Design in an Educational Game-Based Learning Environment," *British Journal of Educational Technology* 42, no. 5 (2011): 456–69; Kristan Harris and Denise Reid, "The Influence of Virtual Reality Play on Children's Motivation," *Canadian Journal of Occupational Therapy* 72, no. 1 (2005): 21–30.

12. B. D. Coller and M. J. Scott, "Effectiveness of Using a Video Game to Teach a Course in Mechanical Engineering," *Computers and Education* 53, no. 3 (2009): 900–12; Martin Ebner and Andreas Holzinger, "Successful Implementation of User-Centered Game Based Learning in Higher Education: An Example from Civil Engineering," *Computers and Education* 49, no. 4 (2007): 873–90.

13. Merrilea J. Mayo, "Games for Science and Engineering Education," *Communications of the ACM* 50, no. 7 (2007): 30–35.

14. Jantina Huizenga, Wilfried Admiraal, Sanne Akkerman, and Geert ten Dam, "Mobile Game-Based Learning in Secondary Education: Engagement, Motivation and Learning in a Mobile City Game," *Journal of Computer Assisted Learning* 25, no. 4 (2009): 341.

15. Lippincott, "Learning, Engagement, and Technology," 174.

16. "Number of Online Console Gamers in the United States from 2014 to 2020 (in Millions)," Statista, 2016, https://www.statista.com/statistics/521822/number-of-online-console-gamers-in-the-us; "Number of Tablet Gamers in the United States from 2011 to 2020 (in Millions)," Statista, 2016, https://www.statista.com/statistics/282443/number-of-tablet-gamers-in-the-us.

17. "Distribution of Computer and Video Gamers in the United States from 2006 to 2016, by Gender," Statista, 2016, https://www.statista.com/statistics/232383/gender-split-of-us-computer-and-video-gamers.

18. Kirby Deater-Deckard, Mido Chang, and Michael E. Evans, "Engagement State and Learning from Educational Games," in *Digital Games: A Context for Cognitive Development,* New Directions for Child and Adolescent Development 139, ed. Fran C. Blumber and Shalom M. Fisch (San Francisco: Jossey Bass, 2013), 27.

19. James Paul Gee, *What Video Games Have to Teach Us about Learning and Literacy* (New York: Palgrave Macmillan, 2003).

20. Mayo, "Games for Science and Engineering Education."

21. Federation of American Scientists, *Summit on Educational Games* (Washington, DC: Federation of American Scientists, 2006), 18–20

22. Daphne Bavelier, C. Shawn Green, Alexandre Pouget, and Paul Schrater, "Brain Plasticity through the Lifespan: Learning to Learn and Action Video Games," *Annual Review of Neuroscience* 35 (2012): 391–416; C. Shawn Green and Daphne Bavelier, "Action Video Game Modifies Visual Selective Attention," *Nature* 423, no. 6939 (2003): 534–38; C. Shawn Green, Alexandre Pouget, and Daphne Bavelier, "Improved Probabilistic Inference as a General Learning Mechanism with Action Video Games," *Current Biology* 20, no. 17 (2010): 1573–79.

23. Guillen-Nieto and Aleson-Carbonell, "Serious Games and Learning Effectiveness," 438.

24. Yaman and Covington, *I'll Take Learning for 500*, 12.
25. Aldrich, *Learning Online*.
26. Kim, "Harnessing the Power," 466.
27. Guy J. Leach and Tammy Sugarman, "Play to Win! Using Games in Library Instruction to Enhance Student Learning," *Research Strategies* 20, no. 3 (2005): 200.
28. Eric Klopfer, Scot Osterweil, Jennifer Groff, and Jason Haas, *The Instructional Power of Digital Games, Social Networking, and Simulations and How Teachers Can Leverage Them* (Cambridge, MA: Massachusetts Institute of Technology, The Education Arcade, 2009), 9.

Bibliography

Aldrich, Clark. *Learning Online with Games, Simulation, and Virtual Worlds*. San Francisco: Jossey-Bass, 2009.

Bavelier, Daphne, C. Shawn Green, Alexandre Pouget, and Paul Schrater. "Brain Plasticity through the Lifespan: Learning to Learn and Action Video Games." *Annual Review of Neuroscience* 35 (2012): 391–416.

Boot, Walter R., Arthur F. Kramer, Daniel J. Simons, Monica Fabiana, and Gabriele Gratton. "The Effects of Video Game Playing on Attention, Memory, and Executive Control." *Acta Psychologica* 129 (2008): 387–98.

Burguillo, Juan C. "Using Game Theory and Competition-Based Learning to Stimulate Student Motivation and Performance." *Computers and Education* 55, no. 2 (2010): 566–75.

Coller, B. D., and M. J. Scott. "Effectiveness of Using a Video Game to Teach a Course in Mechanical Engineering." *Computers and Education* 53, no. 3 (2009): 900–12.

Deater-Deckard, Kirby, Mido Chang, and Michael E. Evans. "Engagement State and Learning from Educational Games." In *Digital Games: A Context for Cognitive Development*. New Directions for Child and Adolescent Development 139. Edited by Fran C. Blumber and Shalom M. Fisch, 21–30. San Francisco: Jossey Bass, 2013.

Dickey, Michele D. "Murder on Grimm Isle: The Impact of Game Narrative Design in an Educational Game-Based Learning Environment." *British Journal of Educational Technology* 42, no. 5 (2011): 456–69.

Ebner, Martin, and Andreas Holzinger. "Successful Implementation of User-Centered Game Based Learning in Higher Education: An Example from Civil Engineering." *Computers and Education* 49, no. 4 (2007): 873–90.

Federation of American Scientists. *Summit on Educational Games: Harnessing the Power of Video Games for Learning*. Washington, DC: Federation of American Scientists, 2006.

Gee, James Paul. *What Video Games Have to Teach Us about Learning and Literacy*. New York: Palgrave Macmillan, 2003.

Green, C. Shawn, and Daphne Bavelier. "Action Video Game Experience Alters the Spatial Resolution of Attention." *Psychological Science* 18, no. 1 (2007): 88–94.

———. "Action Video Game Modifies Visual Selective Attention." *Nature* 423, no. 6939 (2003): 534–38.

Green, C. Shawn, Alexandre Pouget, and Daphne Bavelier. "Improved Probabilistic Inference as a General Learning Mechanism with Action Video Games." *Current Biology* 20, no. 17 (2010): 1573–79.

Greenfield, Patricia M., Luigia Camaioni, Paola Ercolani, Laura Weiss, Bennett A. Lauber, and Paola Perucchini. "Cognitive Socialization by Computer Games in Two Cultures: Inductive Discovery or Mastery of an Iconic Code?" *Journal of Applied Developmental Psychology* 15, no. 1 (1994): 59–85.

Guillen-Nieto, Victoria, and Marian Aleson-Carbonell. "Serious Games and Learning Effectiveness: The Case of It's a Deal!" *Computers and Education* 58, no. 1 (2012): 435–48.

Harris, Kristan, and Denise Reid. "The Influence of Virtual Reality Play on Children's Motivation." *Canadian Journal of Occupational Therapy* 72, no. 1 (2005): 21–30.

Huizenga, Jantina, Wilfried Admiraal, Sanne Akkerman, and Geert ten Dam. "Mobile Game-Based Learning in Secondary Education: Engagement, Motivation and Learning in a Mobile City Game." *Journal of Computer Assisted Learning* 25, no. 4 (2009): 332–44.

Hwang, Gwo-Jen, and Po-Han Wu. "Advancements and Trends in Digital Game-Based Learning Research: A Review of Publications in Selected Journals from 2001 to 2010." *British Journal of Educational Technology* 43, no. 1 (2012): E6–E10.

Karle, James W., Scott Watter, and Judith M. Shedden. "Task Switching in Video Game Players: Benefits of Selective Attention but Not Resistance to Proactive Interference." *Acta Psychologica* 134, no. 1 (2010): 70–78.

Kim, Bohyun. "Harnessing the Power of Game Dynamics." *College and Research Libraries News* 73, no. 8 (2012): 465–69.

Klopfer, Eric, Scot Osterweil, Jennifer Groff, and Jason Haas. *The Instructional Power of Digital Games, Social Networking, and Simulations and How Teachers Can Leverage Them.* Cambridge, MA: Massachusetts Institute of Technology, The Education Arcade, 2009.

Leach, Guy J., and Tammy Sugarman. "Play to Win! Using Games in Library Instruction to Enhance Student Learning." *Research Strategies* 20, no. 3 (2005): 191–203.

Lippincott, Joan K. "Learning, Engagement, and Technology." Chapter 9 in *Student Engagement and Information Literacy.* Edited by Craig Gibson. Chicago: Association of College and Research Libraries, 2006.

Mayo, Merrilea J. "Games for Science and Engineering Education." *Communications of the ACM* 50, no. 7 (2007): 30–35.

Okagaki, Lynn, and Peter Frensch. "Effects of Video Game Playing on Measures of Spatial Performance: Gender Effects in Late Adolescence." *Journal of Applied Developmental Psychology* 15, no. 1 (1994): 33–58.

Pillay, Hitendra. "An Investigation of the Cognitive Process Engaged in by Recreational Computer Game Players: Implications for Skills of the Future." *Journal of Research on Technology in Education* 34, no. 3 (2002): 336–50.

Prayaga, Lakshmi, and John W. Coffey. "Computer Game Development: An Instructional Strategy to Promote Higher Order Thinking Skills." *Journal of Educational Technology* 5, no. 3 (2008): 40–48.

"Grantland Rice (1880–1954)." In *The Hutchinson Unabridged Encyclopedia with Atlas and Weather Guide,* edited by Helicon. (Helicon, 2016.) Rice, Grantland.

Rice, John. "Assessing Higher Order Thinking in Video Games." *Journal of Technology and Teacher Education,* 15, no. 1 (2007): 87–100.

Schwabe, Gerhard, and Christoph Goth. "Mobile Learning with a Mobile Game: Design and Motivational Effects." *Journal of Computer Assisted Learning* 21, no. 3 (2005): 204–16.

Siddique, Zahed, Chen Ling, Piyamas Roberson, Yunjun Xu, and Xiaojun Geng. "Facilitating Higher-Order Learning through Computer Games." *Journal of Mechanical Design* 135, no. 12 (2013): 121004–10.

Staiano, Amanda E., Anisha A. Abraham, and Sandra L. Calvert. "Competitive versus Cooperative Exergame Play for African American Adolescents' Executive Function Skills: Short-Term Effects in a Long-Term Training Intervention." *Developmental Psychology* 48, no. 2 (2012): 337–42.

Statista. "Distribution of Computer and Video Gamers in the United States from 2006 to 2016, by Gender." 2016. https://www.statista.com/statistics/232383/gender-split-of-us-computer-and-video-gamers.

Statista. "Number of Online Console Gamers in the United States from 2014 to 2020 (in Millions)." 2016. https://www.statista.com/statistics/521822/number-of-online-console-gamers-in-the-us.

Statista. "Number of Tablet Gamers in the United States from 2011 to 2020 (in Millions)." 2016. https://www.statista.com/statistics/282443/number-of-tablet-gamers-in-the-us.

VanDeventer, Stephanie S., and James A. White. "Expert Behavior in Children's Video Game Play." *Simulation and Gaming* 33, no. 1 (2002): 28–48.

Yaman, Dan, and Missy Covington. *I'll Take Learning for 500: Using Game Shows to Engage, Motivate, and Train.* San Francisco: Pfeiffer, 2006.

CHAPTER 5

Group Work

Nothing new that is really interesting comes without collaboration.[1]

If you have ever seen *Apollo 13,* you will be familiar with the scene where mission control dumps a box of materials on a table and everyone starts working to figure out how the pieces can be used to fix the space capsule and get the astronauts home. What follows is a buzz of activity as people share ideas and expertise to solve this critical problem. There was no trophy or personal reward for those in the control room, but as a group they were able to work together and accomplish something wonderful. Groups have that power to unite diverse individuals into something more powerful than the individual parts.

Benefits of Groups
Intellectual

In the most basic terms, groups provide their members with more to work with. All individuals bring with them past experiences, ideas, skills, and goals. The end result of this interaction is more than the sum of the parts. This occurs as comments by one member can lead to a new idea by another, which is put into action by the third. Each of these members has contributed something to the group for the betterment of everyone.

Groups allow for the development of in-depth critical thinking and inquiry skills. When working in groups, it is important for members to be able to ask for clarification, critique others, analyze assumptions and implications, and gather perspectives. Teamwork also promotes the development of skills such as being able to develop goals and create a plan, using the strengths of various team members, and placing a topic within a larger context.

Social

As it is impossible to create groups without interacting with other people, there are bound to be social benefits of groups. These are skills that are developed through collaborative work, but that also must be present for groups to be successful. These skills include interpersonal (congenial, positive communication, listening, clear communication, eye contact), group building (organization, staying on task, managing a meeting, empathy), conflict management (prevention, resolution, and mediation), and presentation (summarization, synthesis, report writing, and public speaking).

Often within successful groups, the work and leadership responsibilities rotate through the members based on their individual strengths and knowledge. The ability to take the lead when necessary and allow others to lead in turn is a very helpful skill to have. It shows strength of character to not always have to be the official leader and have everyone follow your direction.

Groups in the Classroom
History and Structure

Working in groups has a very long history within education as well as in everyday life. Humans are pack animals and have flourished by combining and forming into tribes. We have worked together to do things that would be impossible individually. Within the educational setting, group work goes by a number of different terms: collaborative learning, cooperative learning, team-based learning, and learning communities. Within the literature on this topic, there are some mixed definitions of the various terms. Following are some of the more commonly used definitions.

- **Collaborative learning**—a structure that requires students and instructors to work together in order to create knowledge. Students are given more flexibility in collaborative learning. Collaborative learning is often the term used in relation to higher education.

- **Cooperative learning**—the use of small groups in which students work together to maximize their own learning and the learning of their group mates. Within cooperative learning, instructors maintain their role of authority on the subject matter. Cooperative learning is often used when discussing K–12 education.

- **Team-based learning**—the structured use of small teams involving preparation outside of class and then application of the content during class time. A set structure of reading, individual tests, group tests, and discussion is followed for each unit or module covered by the class.

- **Learning communities**—a group of students who work together to achieve a shared academic goal. Learning communities are often made up of more students than those in other group work situations. A learning community may consist of an entire class or individuals pursuing a specific degree. Learning communities also function as long-term groups lasting throughout a semester or longer.

These definitions demonstrate the fact that group learning can be structured to reach different goals based on a variety of educational theories; however, they all seek "to engage students actively in their own learning and to do so in a supportive and challenging social context."[2] Within this book, the term *group work* will be used as a catch-all to include all the different definitions and to avoid any specific procedures related to the different uses of the terms. The literature describes benefits related to all types of group work, and thus no one variation will be promoted over the others. When mentioning different research articles, the terminology set out by the individual authors will be used. Also, given the situation that many librarians see classes for only a limited time, they are not able to fully develop the requirements of some of the various applications of group work.

One method of differentiating groups is by the amount of time that they are expected to work together.

- **Informal groups** are created on an ad hoc basis and work together from a couple of minutes to a full class period. These types of groups do best when they have a focused exercise to complete. This exercise could be a short introduction, transition, or review of a topic.

- **Formal groups** last over several class periods and require the students to work together on a larger product. These groups must connect both within and outside of class in order to achieve the learning objectives.

- Finally, **cooperative groups** are created very specifically by taking into account the different group members' characteristics. They work together throughout an entire course or beyond. These groups require commitment by all individuals involved to complete a variety of tasks. There are a number of subsets within this type of group, ranging from a group established by an instructor for one course up to learning communities developed by the institution that place students in a common set of courses and dorms.

Group work has been used at all age levels for all disciplines. It is one of the most common types of instructional techniques and is also the basis for other instructional methods such as problem-based learning and service learning. There are also a number of specific group learning methods that have been developed by researchers and developed into specific programs to be used in the classroom including these listed by Slavin: Learning Together (LT), Academic Controversy (AC), Student-Team-Achievement-Divisions (STAD), Teams-Games-Tournaments (TGT), Group Investigation (GI), Jigsaw, Team-Accelerated-Instruction (TAI), Peer Assisted Learning Strategies (PALS), and Cooperative Integrated Reading and Composition (CIRC).[3]

There are various theoretical structures relating to why collaborative learning provides such a strong backing for learning in general. Motivational theories such as behavioral learning theory focus on the belief that students will work successfully in groups due to the rewards and goal structure set up within the system. Cognitive theories focus on the effects of working together. One example is Cognitive Developmental theory, which stems from work done by Piaget and Vygotsky noting the importance of working together with more accomplished individuals in order to scaffold understanding through the Zone of Proximal Development. The second cognitive theory is Cognitive Elaboration theory, which notes that for learning to occur, the information must be engaged with by the learner. Group work allows for interaction with content through a variety of ways as people work together reading, writing, and summarizing in order to offer explanations to other group members.

One of the important pedagogical underpinnings of group work corresponds to student-centered learning. When implementing group work in the classroom, the focus shifts from the instructor to the students themselves. It is the students who must interact and work with the content rather than having the instructor provide it to them.

Research Studies

The intellectual and social benefits of groups can also be seen in the class-room. A meta-analysis of hundreds of research studies on cooperative learning methods conducted by Johnson, Johnson, and Stanne found higher individual achievement is obtained through cooperative learning when compared to individualistic or competitive classrooms.[4] Johnson, Johnson, and Smith found within their review of research studies that positive results were found in "promoting meta-cognitive thought, willingness to take on difficult tasks, persistence (despite difficulties) in working toward goal accomplishment, intrinsic motivation, transfer of learning from one situation to another, and greater time on task."[5] In relation to intellectual growth, cooperative learning is more effective than traditional approaches, such as lectures, in improving critical thinking, advanced cognitive development, and higher academic achievement.[6] Davis notes that "researchers report that, regardless of the subject matter, students working in small teams tend to learn more of what is taught and retain it longer than when the same content is presented in other instructional formats."[7]

Slavin found in his review of the literature a number of benefits beyond academic achievement, including intergroup relations, self-esteem, proacademic peer norms, positive locus of control, time on task, classroom behavior, liking of class and school, liking classmates and feeling liked by classmates, cooperation, altruism, and the ability to take on another's perspective.[8] Positive social benefits include increased positive relationships between heterogeneous students, increased self-esteem, self-efficacy, social competencies, coping skills, and positive attitudes toward school.[9]

Sweet and Pelton-Sweet note how a student's social connection in the classroom affects "academic performance, self-efficacy, motivation to learn, and perceptions of one's instructor, peers, and task value."[10] Yaman and Covington show that the benefits of group work increase collaboration and participation, create a bond between members, limit the potential embarrassment of answering questions individually, hold group members equally accountable, and allow members to learn from and teach one another.[11] The last of these benefits—learning from and teaching one another—goes beyond the matter of course content; group dynamics also facilitate the exchange of diversity in culture, ideas, and beliefs. As Sutton, Zamora, and Best state, "Within groups, students teach and learn from one another—they share insights, model skills, and probe each other's thoughts."[12]

Instructional Benefits

The nature of group work corresponds directly to the research that is done examining the characteristics of successful classrooms. Astin found that student-student interactions and student-faculty interactions were the most important influences on academic success and satisfaction.[13] This interaction is the central aspect of group work. Group work also fits in with the Seven Principles for Good Practice in Undergraduate Education. Three of the seven principles in particular are readily addressed by group work: contact between students and faculty, cooperation among students, and active learning.[14]

Group work allows students to hear ideas and perspectives from a variety of positions, which allows for the development of deeper understanding of topics. It is also helpful for students to discuss topics in groups, as they are able to use language that is understandable to each other. An instructor may unconsciously use terms or examples that do not relate to students, while students are able to connect with each other as peers.

Students taking part in group work also have the opportunity to develop a positive relationship with learning by establishing study habits and an opening, questioning relationship with the course content. Putting students together in groups allows them to share interest in a topic, which will optimally result in deeper interaction and more meaningful learning.

Group work allows for students with different levels of understanding to interact with each other around a topic. This promotes the use of Vygotsky's Zone of Proximal Development. This means that students with a lower understanding will benefit from the understanding of higher students. This mix of students also benefits the higher level students as they share with the other students. Teaching a topic to someone else has been frequently shown as a way to increase understanding. This means that group work provides benefits for all types of students.

Group work also provides a positive impact on retention and persistence, another important consideration for higher education.[15] This effect stems from the fact that connection and interaction with others on campus is one of the big drivers in students staying on campus. If students feel connected with someone at the institution, they are more likely to stay.

Successful Group Work

The quality of learning undertaken by groups can vary depending on a number of factors. Meyers and Jones put forth five features that should be in place for successful collaborative learning:

- A sense of **interdependence** among team members. Team members should believe that their success depends upon the success of their teammates.
- **Accountability** of individual students to both team and instructor. While team members depend on one another, they are also accountable for their own learning. This means they will be evaluated both for their work in the team and as individuals.
- Frequent **face-to-face interaction** to promote team goals. Teams must not simply divide up the learning task and work on it in isolation; they must interact and focus on the task.
- Development of **social skills** needed for collaboration. Group work requires the development of specific social skills. Instructors must promote the development of these skills as well as knowledge in the content area.
- **Critical analysis** of group processes. Teams need to reflect on the work they are doing during and after the group work. This reflection relates both to the course content and to the workings of the group.[16]

A pretty typical subpar group assignment puts students into a group to write a paper. At this point, the students divide up the paper and each goes off to work individually. They have a deadline set to get their work to someone who puts it all together. At least one person misses this deadline, and there is an e-mail exchange trying to get that part of the paper completed. In the meantime, someone is putting the paper together by maybe adding a transition sentence between the sections written individually. They usually get the formatting fixed, ensuring that the font and spacing is the same throughout, but there is no consideration for the flow, structure, or cohesiveness of the work. If they get the missing section, it will be thrown in at the end. If not, the person who organized the paper will quickly type something in order make sure everything is covered. The paper is handed in with the group getting one grade.

Based on this experience, there is always a group member who is resentful that others got the same grade and did little to no work. This member approaches future group work with the idea that group work just means more work in order to help out an undeserving classmate. There is also a group member who was able to coast by with little work. This member approaches future group work with the goal of finding a "smart classmate" who will help the rest of the group receive a better grade. There are finally the group members who did the bare minimum in order to get the project done. These members approach future group work doing just what is necessary to get by. Overall, none of these students has engaged with the topic or is able to fully implement what they were supposed to learn. They could have each written their own paper with a resulting range of quality. Instead, the instructor has a collection of similar papers that each possesses the same disjointed and uneven writing.

This example has failed to meet any of the features of successful group work. First, success within the paper did not require interdependence among the group. There was no need for each group member to learn about and understand the entire topic. Second, each member got the same grade for the paper. This meant that there was no individual accountability. It was possible for a member to contribute nothing to the group. Third, the group did not need to interact. They were able to complete the paper apart from one another. Fourth, there was no need for or development of social skills. Social skills would have helped with communication for the members to share how they felt. Finally, the group did not analyze the process. They were not able to think about and discuss the process of completing the paper, which means that they had no way to work through what turned out to be a negative process.

When initiating group work within the classroom, be sure to consider how these features will be met. While some elements, such as having individual and group accountability in regard to grades, will not be applicable for librarians teaching a single session class, it is still important to make sure that both individuals and the group are equally responsible, rather than one or two individuals in the group taking on all the work and responsibility.

Groups and Technology

Integrating technology into group work can take a number of forms, but each should address the features of successful group work discussed previously. Within face-to-face sessions, technology can be used as a tool allowing group members to work together on an individual project. While there are a number of cooperative technologies with an ever-changing array of features and offerings, one common location is Google with a range of tools that allow a wide number of individuals to work on the same item at the same time. It is best to use well-known products when working with students in a short time frame. During semester-long courses, it is possible to have students sign up for product accounts with lesser known or more specific features.

These cooperative technologies are not only useful when teaching face-to-face sessions, but also when developing group work for online sessions. Integrating group work within an online class poses a new set of challenges. When embedded within a course offered by another faculty member, the librarian must work closely with that individual in order to promote group work that fits within the pedagogical structure developed by the faculty member. If group work is not a part of the overall course, it is harder to integrate it online as opposed to in person. Even within a semester-length class, it can be difficult to establish group work. Kleinsasser and Hong provide a look at the challenges in setting up group work within an online environment as well as offering a design on how to develop meaningful group discussions within a course management system.[17]

Considerations

Given the limitations of single-session instruction, librarians may not have the amount of time needed to provide students with the necessary guidelines and support for establishing ideal groups. However, the increased use of group work in higher education means that students will likely have some experience with the concept and be able to work effectively with team members for the purpose of completing short instructional tasks. One of the most common activities used by library instructors is Think, Pair, Share, which involves the creation of small, ad hoc student groups that are asked questions and required to discuss their answers with teammates before responding to the entire class. This type of group activity helps to generate new ideas and prevents classroom discussion from being dominated by a few individuals.

Group work is often discussed in relation to the fact that it offers a change from the individual competitive nature that is found in many classrooms. In the traditional classroom, students compete against each other in order to get the right answer and demonstrate their superior knowledge over other students. They may also be competing for a limited number of As and Bs. This approach leads to students hoarding information because by sharing their knowledge they are losing their edge over others. Collaborative work requires students to work together and interact with the content on multiple levels. This interaction leads to increased understanding. Even though the literature notes some of the downsides of a purely competitive classroom in relation to learning, it does not call for a complete abandonment of competition or individual work.

In fact, competition can be combined well with group work. Using this system, groups work together to compete with other teams. This structure provides support and assistance that is not found in individual competition. Group competition also results in additional enjoyment as the group mates are able to bond and support each other's accomplishments. They are also able to support each other in case of failure, as there is a decrease in individual responsibility for failure, which results in lower negativity. Often even after a defeat, the group unity is such that members will support each other and praise the work that was done.

When group work is initiated in the classroom, it must be evaluated with conscious consideration as to its benefits and effectiveness. First, it must make sense for the students to be working in groups. Merely having students sit in "groups" while working on a project does not automatically result in the benefits of group work. There must be a specific reason for the students to be in a group as opposed to doing the work individually. In addition to having a reason to be in a group, it is also important that each person have a say in the group. The goal in group work is to have every member understand the content; this means that each member of the group must be able to articulate and use the content by working with it in their group. Group work is not effective if only one person understands and does the work without the others.

One method of ensuring that all the members of the group understand the content can be accomplished through the report out. Have the groups figure out the answer or discuss the issue, but when it is time to report back to the rest of the class on their findings, do not let them choose who will talk. Rather, a random person from the group will be called. This means that everyone must understand, because they do not know in advance who will have to talk for the group. When a random person is chosen to talk, it is also important that the students understand that it is random and that you are not picking on specific individuals. One method would be to have a number assigned to each individual and then choose a number out of a hat. Some instructors also use playing cards to pick randomly.

Instructors also need to remember that students likely have had experiences with groups that were not successful. They may have had a group member that just freeloaded off the work of the others or who would not listen to what anyone else said and made all the decisions. In cases such as these, the negative experience may have soured future encounters with group work. These poor experiences were the result of mismanagement on the part of the instructor. It may therefore be helpful before you initiate group work to explain to the class why you are having them form groups and what their responsibilities will be. This lets them know that you are not just giving them time to talk to one another; rather, you have the expectation that they will learn and apply the content.

Intrinsic Motivational Factors

As noted in chapter 1, there are seven factors that promote intrinsic motivation. Group work addresses the following factors:

- **Competition**—Some group work places the groups in opposition to each other to reach a goal. It also occurs that even when there is no competition, some groups may create their own competition by playfully claiming to be better than the other groups. This provides a group unity by creating an "us against them" mentality.
- **Cooperation**—Group work is based on the idea of cooperation: that by working together, the individuals are all able to achieve the set goal.
- **Recognition**—By working together, individuals are able to have their group mates see their contributions. They are recognized for what they bring to the group.
- **Control**—Group work often allows the members choices as to how they will split up the work and who will take on what roles. This option of control lets them take ownership of the group's work.

Conclusion

The group work lesson plans offered in part II of this book will focus on informal groups. Stein and Hurd note several instances when informal learning teams can be successfully utilized.[18] These include **introductory exercises** used to engage student interest, **transitional exercises** used to shift from lecture to discussion as a way to stimulate participation and gauge the understanding of the students, and **review sessions** used to provide students with a chance to form and clarify their understanding.

When groups are used properly to motivate students to engage with the subject content by having them work together to create understanding, they have been proven successful across all age levels and in all disciplines. The intellectual benefits of group work, including enhanced critical thinking and evaluation, fit perfectly with the *Framework for Information*

Literacy. Given these results and benefits, librarians should take time to incorporate group work within their instruction sessions. Well-planned-out group work is a strong addition to the range of instructional techniques that can be applied in the classroom.

Notes

1. Johnson, David W. 2015. *Constructive controversy: theory, research, practice.* New York: Cambridge University Press, 2015. 169.
2. Elizabeth F. Barkley, K. Patricia Cross, and Claire Howell Major, *Collaborative Learning Techniques* (San Francisco: Jossey-Bass, 2005), 9.
3. Robert E. Slavin, *Cooperative Learning* (Boston: Allyn and Bacon, 1995).
4. David W. Johnson, Roger T. Johnson, and Mary Beth Stanne, "Cooperative Learning Methods: A Meta-Analysis," Cooperative Learning Center at the University of Minnesota, May 2000, http://www.clcrc.com/pages/cl-methods.html (site now discontinued).
5. David W. Johnson, Roger T. Johnson, and Karl A. Smith, "Cooperative Learning Returns to College," *Change* 30, no. 4 (1998): 31.
6. James S. Cooper, L. Prescott, L. Cook, L. Smith, R. Mueck, and J. Cuseo, *Cooperative Learning and College Instruction* (Long Beach: California State University Foundation, 1990); Leonard Springer, Mary Elizabeth Stanne, and Samuel Donovan, "Effects of Small-Group Learning on Undergraduates in Science, Mathematics, Engineering, and Technology: A Meta-analysis," *Review of Educational Research* 69, no. 1 (1999): 50–80; David W. Johnson and Roger T. Johnson, "The Socialization and Achievement Crisis: Are Cooperative Learning Experiences the Solution?" in *Applied Social Psychology Annual: Applied Social Psychology and Education: v. 4,* ed. Leonard B. Bickman (Newbury Park, CA: Sage, 1983) 119-164; Robert E. Slavin, "When Does Cooperative Learning Increase Student Achievement?" *Psychological Bulletin* 94, no. 3 (1983): 429–45; Sharon J. Hamilton-Wieler, *Collaboration: See Treason* (Bloomington, IN: National Council of Teachers of English, 1992); Sharon Hamilton and Edmund Hansen, *Sourcebook for Collaborative Learning in the Arts and Sciences at Indiana University* (Bloomington: Indiana University, 1992).
7. Barbara Gross Davis, *Tools for Teaching* (San Francisco: Jossey-Bass, 1993), 147.
8. Slavin, *Cooperative Learning.*
9. David W. Johnson and Roger T. Johnson, *Cooperation and Competition* (Edina, MN: Interaction Book Company, 1989); Johnson, Johnson, and Smith, "Cooperative Learning Returns to College."
10. Michael Sweet and Laura Pelton-Sweet, "The Social Foundation of Team-Based Learning: Students Accountable to Students," in *Team-Based Learning: Small-Group Learning's Next Big Step,* ed. Larry K. Michaelsen, Michael Sweet, and Dean X. Parmelee (San Francisco: Jossey-Bass, 2008), 29.
11. Dan Yaman and Missy Covington, *I'll Take Learning for 500* (San Francisco: Pfeiffer, 2006), 11.
12. Mark Sutton, Mia Zamora, and Linda Best, "Practical Insights on the Pedagogy of Group Work," *Research and Teaching in Developmental Education* 22, no. 1 (2005): 77.

13. Alexander Astin, *What Matters in College* (San Francisco: Jossey-Bass, 1993).
14. Arthur W. Chickering and Zelda F. Gamson, "Seven Principles for Good Practice in Undergraduate Education," *American Association for Higher Education Bulletin* 39 (1987): 3–7.
15. Philip U. Treisman, "A Study of the Mathematics Performance of Black Students at the University of California, Berkeley" (PhD thesis, University of California, Berkeley, 1985).
16. Chet Meyers and Thomas B. Jones, *Promoting Active Learning Strategies for the College Classroom* (San Francisco: Jossey-Bass, 1993).
17. Robert Kleinsasser and Yi-chun Hong, "Online Group Work Design: Processes, Complexities, and Intricacies," *TechTrends* 60, no. 6 (2016): 569–76.
18. Ruth Federman Stein and Sandra Hurd, *Using Student Teams in the Classroom* (Bolton, MA: Anker Publishing, 2000).

Bibliography

Astin, Alexander. *What Matters in College: Four Critical Years Revisited.* San Francisco: Jossey-Bass, 1993.

Barkley, Elizabeth F., K. Patricia Cross, and Claire Howell Major. *Collaborative Learning Techniques.* San Francisco: Jossey-Bass, 2005.

Chickering, Arthur W., and Zelda F. Gamson. "Seven Principles for Good Practice in Undergraduate Education." *American Association for Higher Education Bulletin* 39 (1987): 3–7.

Cooper, James S., L. Prescott, L. Cook, L. Smith, R. Mueck, and J. Cuseo. *Cooperative Learning and College Instruction: Effective Use of Student Learning Teams.* Long Beach: California State University Foundation, 1990.

Davis, Barbara Gross. *Tools for Teaching.* San Francisco: Jossey-Bass, 1993.

Hamilton, Sharon, and Edmund Hansen. *Sourcebook for Collaborative Learning in the Arts and Sciences at Indiana University.* Bloomington: Indiana University, 1992.

Hamilton-Wieler, Sharon J. *Collaboration: See Treason: Report of a Three-Year Study of Collaborative Learning in Freshman Composition Classrooms.* Bloomington, IN: National Council of Teachers of English, 1992.

Johnson, David W. 2015. *Constructive controversy: theory, research, practice.* New York: Cambridge University Press, 2015. 169.

Johnson, David W., and Roger T. Johnson. *Cooperation and Competition: Theory and Research.* Edina, MN: Interaction Book Company, 1989.

———. "The Socialization and Achievement Crisis: Are Cooperative Learning Experiences the Solution?" In *Applied Social Psychology Annual: Applied Social Psychology and Education: v. 4.* Edited by Leonard B. Bickman, 119-164. Newbury Park, CA: Sage, 1983.

Johnson, David W., Roger T. Johnson, and Karl A. Smith. "Cooperative Learning Returns to College." *Change* 30, no. 4 (1998): 26–35.

Johnson, David W., Roger T. Johnson, and Mary Beth Stanne. "Cooperative Learning Methods: A Meta-analysis." Cooperative Learning Center at the University of Minnesota, May 2000. http://www.clcrc.com/pages/cl-methods.html (site now discontinued).

Kleinsasser, Robert, and Yi-chun Hong. "Online Group Work Design: Processes, Complexities, and Intricacies." *TechTrends* 60, no. 6 (2016): 569–76.

Meyers, Chet, and Thomas B. Jones. *Promoting Active Learning Strategies for the College Classroom.* San Francisco: Jossey-Bass, 1993.

Slavin, Robert E. *Cooperative Learning.* Boston: Allyn and Bacon, 1995.

———. "When Does Cooperative Learning Increase Student Achievement?" *Psychological Bulletin* 94, no. 3 (1983): 429–45.

Springer, Leonard, Mary Elizabeth Stanne, and Samuel Donovan. "Effects of Small-Group Learning on Undergraduates in Science, Mathematics, Engineering, and Technology: A Meta-analysis." *Review of Educational Research* 69, no. 1 (1999): 50–80.

Stein, Ruth Federman, and Sandra Hurd. *Using Student Teams in the Classroom.* Bolton, MA: Anker Publishing, 2000.

Sutton, Mark, Mia Zamora, and Linda Best. "Practical Insights on the Pedagogy of Group Work." *Research and Teaching in Developmental Education* 22, no. 1 (2005): 71–81.

Sweet, Michael, and Laura Pelton-Sweet. "The Social Foundation of Team-Based Learning: Students Accountable to Students." In *Team-Based Learning: Small-Group Learning's Next Big Step.* Edited by Larry K. Michaelsen, Michael Sweet, and Dean X. Parmelee, 119-164. San Francisco: Jossey-Bass, 2008.

Treisman, Philip U. "A Study of the Mathematics Performance of Black Students at the University of California, Berkeley." PhD thesis, University of California, Berkeley, 1985.

Yaman, Dan, and Missy Covington. *I'll Take Learning for 500: Using Game Shows to Engage, Motivate, and Train.* San Francisco: Pfeiffer, 2006.

PART II
Fun as a Means of Motivation

The next part of this book will provide a range of lesson plans addressing the three instructional techniques discussed in part I. Each chapter addresses one of the six threshold concepts set out in the *Framework for Information Literacy for Higher Education*. Within each chapter, there will be three lesson plans, one each focusing on humor, group work, and games. Although the lesson plans are all connected with one of the three learning techniques, they often overlap with the other techniques. It can be hard to play a game without humor creeping in. And some students will turn any group work into a competitive challenge by declaring their group the winner even if the work was not a game.

Lesson plans should be created with a backward design approach that first calls for the development of the learning outcome. This step requires the instructor to identify what the students should know or be able to do at the end of the lesson. This corresponds to the learning objective noted in the lesson plans. Next, the instructor should calculate how to determine when the students have reached this learning objective. What evidence will they provide or create to show their understanding? This corresponds to the assessments applied in the lesson plans. The final step addresses the instructional strategy required to reach the learning outcome, which will include the activities and instructional experiences. This corresponds to the procedure section noted in the lesson plans. A classic text on backward design is *Understanding by Design* by Wiggins and McTighe.[1] This publication has provided structure for a number of individuals planning instruction sessions. Those looking for a text that addresses more in-depth concepts of instructional design can consult *Real World Instructional Design* by Cennamo and Kalk.[2]

Each of the sample lessons in this section starts with a short summary stating its purpose. Next follows a learning objective. Learning objectives are the foundation of any instruction session, as they provide the stated aim behind the instruction. They set out what students will do in order to reach a specific instructional goal. Learning objectives also provide a structure for student assessment, as the assessment tool must focus on the stated learning objectives.

These learning objectives were developed in order to highlight an ability or knowledge addressed by the corresponding threshold concept. The task force that developed the new *Framework for Information Literacy for Higher Education* states that "neither the knowledge practices/abilities nor the dispositions are intended to be used as learning outcomes."[3] Rather, it is up to each institution to develop outcomes that correspond to the needs and standards of the institution. Mastery of the threshold concepts laid out in the *Framework* requires extended time, practice, and application of the central ideas. As a result, it is not possible to write one learning objective to encompass an entire concept. However, parts of any individual concept can be addressed within various learning objectives. Oakleaf provides a well-laid-out approach for those looking to write learning objectives for the new threshold concepts found in the *Framework*.[4] One of the important points of her article is that the best way to address and assess learning objectives based on threshold concepts is through the use of active learning strategies in which the students are required to do something to demonstrate their knowledge. This strategy is incorporated as much as possible into the lesson plans developed in the second half of this book.

These lesson plans address a range of student abilities in order to provide examples that might work for the wide range of instruction sessions offered by librarians. Some lessons are meant for individuals first entering college, while others would be more applicable to graduate students. The lessons also try to address different class sizes, from small seminars to large lecture classes.

The procedure of the lesson plan provides a step-by-step outline for implementation. This outline includes the approximate time required to go through the lesson; any supplies that are needed; and, as applicable, a script for the librarian to read, rules for a game, or suggested guidelines for what the students and librarian should do during the lesson.

The next aspect of each lesson plan addresses assessment. This is a critical component of every instruction session. Assessment is a continual process, the aim of which is to find out whether the students are meeting the stated learning objectives. The results of these assessments then can influence any changes that are made subsequently in the instruction offered. This process continues with more effective instruction and enhanced learning within each successive round of the cycle.

The importance of assessment derives from two main areas. First, on the individual level, it is important for instructors to know that their students are meeting the learning goals that have been set up for them. Assessment in this way allows the instructor to determine the effectiveness of the instruction. On an institutional level, assessment is becoming a critical component as colleges and universities work to demonstrate the effect they are having on their students to a range of stakeholders including accreditation agencies; local, state, and federal governing bodies; and students themselves.

The sample lesson plans offer assessment measures for both formative and summative assessment. **Formative assessment** is assessment that is done throughout the instruction offered to students. It is used as a means of guiding future instruction offered to the same students. Simply put, it is a way to determine whether students understand what is being taught or if the content needs to be addressed in more depth. As formative assessment allows students to "share control of the class with the instructor,"[5] it promotes intrinsic motivation. Formative assessment is typically qualitative feedback that indicates to the instructor how to proceed in the lesson. This often on-the-fly assessment allows the instructor to monitor the understanding of the students. Formative assessment could also be seen as comprehension checks, informing the instructor whether the students are ready to move on to the next topic. Some methods of conducting formative assessment include asking questions of students, monitoring the questions asked by students, or asking students to summarize what they understand.

Summative assessment is assessment that is done at the conclusion of the instruction in order to determine what the students have learned and understood. It can be thought of as a final proof of student comprehension. Summative assessments provide an evaluation of the students' learning in relation to an established goal. Some examples of summative assessment include an exam, paper, or final project. Some of the artifacts used in the summative assessments within the lesson plans in part II could be used as formative assessments within a full-length class. For example, concept maps could be used as a method of gauging the students' understanding before continuing with further instruction. However, given the short instruction sessions often provided by librarians, these items are most often used as the summative assessments at the end of the lessons.

There are a number of methods that can be used to conduct assessments. Effective assessment will use a range of methods in order to get a broad picture of the learning that is taking place. Two broad categories of assessment are indirect measures and direct measures. Indirect measures provide a secondhand view of the learning that has taken place. Some of the most common indirect measures include surveys and course grades.

Direct measures look at learning first hand. Some of the most common direct measures in information literacy assessment are bibliography reviews and research journals or logs. Another source of direct assessment is authentic assessment. Authentic assessment asks students to demonstrate "in a meaningful way, what they know and are able to do."[6] It also looks at the process rather than just the end product. Thus, this type of assessment fits perfectly with the threshold concepts put forth in the *Framework*, as the threshold concepts deal not only with discrete skills but also with how students think about a task. Some types of authentic assessment include rubrics, concept mapping, minute writing, cases, and portfolios. Jacobson and Xu offer a more in-depth look at how these assessments can be used.[7]

These lesson plans offer a range of assessment methods. Given their importance, however, as many authentic assessment measures as possible are included, especially the use of rubrics. Information literacy is a discipline that must be continually developed rather than a skill that can be simply mastered. To address this range of development, the rubrics use the language of the *Framework* to detail specific traits and demonstrations categorized as Expert, Intermediate, and Novice Learner. It is not to be expected that each student will reach the point of Expert Learner after these sessions. But by discovering the average understanding of the students, it would be possible to adapt future sessions accordingly. Another authentic assessment method that is useful is minute writing as "students who are asked to engage a learning process that requires writing as demonstration and artifact of their own inquiry are more likely to report both learning and engagement."[8]

Each lesson plan ends with a section on notes, modifications and accommodations. These provide advice or comments related to the lesson plans. This section also provides possible methods for expanding or changing the lesson plans to address diverse audiences. These suggestions are not the only method of modifying the lessons, as these lesson plans are not meant to be the only way to teach students these learning objectives. But it is hoped that they will provide inspiration and some guidance for the instruction librarian to start incorporating various instructional techniques that provide fun into library instruction sessions. The lessons and assessments themselves can be modified as the instructor sees fit in order to meet the stated goals and to meld with the instructor's individual personality. Because if the instructor is not having fun, it is going to be difficult to convince others to have fun.

Notes

1. Grant P. Wiggins and Jay McTighe, *Understanding by Design* (Alexandria, VA: Association for Supervision and Curriculum Development, 1998).
2. Katherine Cennamo and Debby Kalk, *Real World Instructional Design* (Belmont, CA: Wadsworth/Thomson Learning, 2005).
3. Megan Oakleaf, "A Roadmap for Assessing Student Learning Using the New Framework for Information Literacy for Higher Education," *Journal of Academic Librarianship* 40, no. 5 (2014): 510.
4. Ibid.
5. Mary J. Snyder Broussard, "Using Games to Make Formative Assessment Fun in the Academic Library," *Journal of Academic Librarianship* 40, no. 1 (2014): 38.
6. Kathleen Montgomery, "Authentic Tasks and Rubrics: Going Beyond Traditional Assessments in College Teaching," *College Teaching* 50, no.1 (2002): 35.
7. Trudi E. Jacobson and Lijuan Xu, "Motivating Students in Credit-Based Information Literacy Courses: Theories and Practice," *portal: Libraries and the Academy* 2, no. 3 (2002): 423-41.
8. Randy Burke Hensley, "Ways of Thinking: Doing Research and Being Information Literate," in *Student Engagement and Information Literacy,* ed. Craig Gibson (Chicago: Association of College and Research Libraries, 2006), 61.

Bibliography

Cennamo, Katherine, and Debby Kalk. *Real World Instructional Design.* Belmont, CA: Wadsworth/Thomson Learning, 2005.

Hensley, Randy Burke. "Ways of Thinking: Doing Research and Being Information Literate." In *Student Engagement and Information Literacy,* edited by Craig Gibson, 55–67. Chicago: Association of College and Research Libraries, 2006.

Jacobson, Trudi E., and Lijuan Xu. "Motivating Students in Credit-Based Information Literacy Courses: Theories and Practice." *portal: Libraries and the Academy* 2, no. 3 (2002): 423–41.

Montgomery, Kathleen. "Authentic Tasks and Rubrics: Going Beyond Traditional Assessments in College Teaching," *College Teaching* 50, no.1 (2002): 34-39.

Oakleaf, Megan. "A Roadmap for Assessing Student Learning Using the New Framework for Information Literacy for Higher Education." *Journal of Academic Librarianship* 40, no. 5 (2014): 510–14.

Snyder Broussard, Mary J. "Using Games to Make Formative Assessment Fun in the Academic Library." *Journal of Academic Librarianship* 40, no. 1 (2014): 35–42.

Wiggins, Grant P., and Jay McTighe. *Understanding by Design*. Alexandria, VA: Association for Supervision and Curriculum Development, 1998.

CHAPTER 6

Framework Concept

Authority Is Constructed and Contextual

Information resources reflect their creators' expertise and credibility and are evaluated based on the information need and the context in which the information will be used. Authority is constructed in that various communities may recognize different types of authority. It is contextual in that the information need may help to determine the level of authority required.[1]

Lesson Plan 1. Humor
Lesson Plan Purpose

This lesson plan offers an **introduction to the topic of authority**. It has students consider what it means to have authority and that popularity does not equal authority.

Learning Objective

Students will discuss the idea of authority in order to understand its importance in relation to context.

Audience

Lower-level undergraduates. Class size from 2 to 200.

Procedures

Time—15 minutes

Supplies—Two example horoscopes. One horoscope should be serious and the other humorous, such as from *The Onion*. Physical copies can be printed for distribution, or an electronic version can be projected. Make sure the horoscopes have the dates by the signs for those who do not know their astrological sign.

Process—Ask the students to close their eyes. Instruct them with their eyes closed to spend twenty seconds thinking about what they will do today and what will happen to them. While their eyes are closed, bring up the serious horoscopes on the screen or pass out the physical copies. After the twenty seconds, have them open their eyes and read their horoscope. It is okay to let them share their horoscopes with each other, as this opens the conversation and reassures them that it is okay to speak in the class. People often like to share their horoscopes. Ask them if their plan for the day has now changed. Have them give reasons why or why not. Note that perhaps they have just not read the right horoscope and then project or share the humorous horoscopes. Again ask them if their plan for the day has changed.

Start a more in-depth discussion by noting that thousands of people read their horoscopes every day. Doesn't that mean that horoscopes are credible and an authoritative resource to use for planning your day? If people are not reading horoscopes to actually decide how to live their life, why are they reading them? How does the purpose and information need change whom you believe? Discussion can continue by asking about the author of the horoscopes. This segues into the idea that often an idea can be shared, but there is no real authority behind the information. This is what happens with rumors, and it is always important to approach something with honest skepticism until it is possible to determine who is advocating a point of view and why they are doing so.

What follows this introduction depends on the individual needs and objectives of the class. Some possible topics that could be addressed next include peer review, evaluation, or ways to determine the qualifications of an authority.

Assessment Opportunities

Formative Assessment—Formative assessment is done through the replies of the students as they discuss why horoscopes are or are not authoritative. An important concept for the students to demonstrate is that there are different information needs, and while someone or some resource may be useful in one situation, it will not be appropriate in all situations.

Summative Assessment—The primary purpose of this lesson plan is to introduce the idea of authority and engage students for further discussion on the topic. Thus, an in-depth summative assessment just on this use of humor will not be possible. It may be possible to include a question on authority within a larger information literacy quiz completed after the instruction session. This would provide data on the understanding of the students relative to the concept of authority. It would also be possible to have the students complete a one-minute paper on the topic of authority. A simple prompt for this writing would be, "How will thinking about authority affect your next search for information?" These papers would be collected and could be assessed using the rubric in table 6.1.

Table 6.1 Rubric for assessing one-minute papers on authority.			
	Expert Learner	**Intermediate Learner**	**Novice Learner**
Clarifies how authority depends on expertise.	Recognizes that an authority on the topic will possess years of experience and/or education and/or an extensive publication history.	Is able to explain how the author/creator had developed their expertise.	States author/creator was expert without further explanation as to how this was determined.

Table 6.1
Rubric for assessing one-minute papers on authority.

	Expert Learner	Intermediate Learner	Novice Learner
Clarifies how authority depends on context.	Articulates how the expertise held by the author/creator is important and fits within the context of the topic/research question.	Notes how authority depends on the context of the research topic but does not describe how authority matches the need of the current topic.	Shows no understanding that authority in one context does not mean authority is held in another context.

Notes/Modifications/Accommodations

It would be possible to explore the use of astrology in other ways during the class to also address the concept of authority. As another example, have the students share their astrological signs. You would then put them together according to the strength of their astrological friendship compatibility. These can be found on different websites; for example, Scorpio goes with Pisces, while Taurus will be most compatible with Cancer. Let them know that they are now best friends with this new person. This results in the humor with some unlikely pairings. This opens up the class to the discussion. Question prompts could include the following: Do you use astrology in deciding on friends? Why or why not? Do you use astrology for anything? In what context does it make sense? Do you know anyone who uses astrology as a guiding authority? Another way to deepen the discussion could be to include the descriptions as to why the two signs should be friends. Individuals often find some similarities to the traits listed in their astrological sign, so it could be asked, if the details are true, why would the whole system lack authority?

It is possible that there may be an individual or several individuals in a particular class who may be very serious with regard to astrology. These students may be offended if all of astrology is brushed off as nonsense. To counter this, it is important to guide the conversation within the structure that relying solely on horoscopes to guide your daily activities and expectations can be a detriment. Horoscopes do not have real authority to tell you what will happen during the day. This can also be a great opportunity to highlight the fact that as individuals, the students are approaching this topic with their own opinions and biases, and this may affect how they respond. It is important to always be aware of personal approaches and contexts in order to construct a complete picture of a topic and those experts within the topic.

Lesson Plan 2. Game
Lesson Plan Purpose

This lesson plan offers a **reinforcement of the topic of authority**. Students are required to show their understanding of authority by looking beyond the most convenient resource in order to find the highest quality resource. In addition to using evaluation skills to select the resource, they must also demonstrate an understanding of evaluation by presenting their resource to explain what makes it authoritative.

Learning Objective

Students will analyze the authority of a source in order to find a high-quality artifact on a specific topic.

Audience

Class size ranging from 6 to 25. Undergraduates through graduate students.

Procedures

Time—50–75 minutes

Supplies—Computer and Internet access for students; preferably each student should have individual access. Projector and screen.

Process—

PURPOSE: Small teams will compete to present the most authoritative artifact (article, website, video, lecture, etc.) on a specific topic. Judging of the artifacts will be done by the librarian and class instructor. The team that is able to make the most compelling case for its artifact will be declared the winner.

INTRODUCTION—LIBRARIAN'S SCRIPT: *Today's game will be a challenge of your searching abilities, your critical thinking skills, and your ability to make a persuasive argument as well as question others' arguments. You will be working in teams using your combined skills, experiences, and knowledge in a game we are calling "Respect My Authority."*

GAME PLAY:

1. Class is broken up into groups of 3–4 students.

2. The entire class is given a research topic or question on which they will focus their research for the game.

3. Students are given free range to find the most authoritative artifact they can on the topic. They are open to using whatever resources they see fit, including open Internet webpages, library resources, etc.

4. When they have selected their artifact, they must prepare a persuasive presentation that highlights the reasons why their artifact is the most authoritative.

5. After approximately 25 minutes, the students will begin their presentations.

6. After each presentation, the other teams will be given an opportunity to ask questions. These questions are meant to really get into the details of the authority of the artifact. Students should be told that asking good questions will result in earning more points for their team, but it may also enable the other teams to make a stronger case for their artifact.

7. After all the presentations, the librarian and instructor consult using their rubrics (table 6.2) to decide which team made the most compelling case for the authority of its artifact.

EXAMPLE TOPICS AND RESEARCH QUESTIONS:

- Existence of extraterrestrial beings.
- How have visits by researchers and tourists affected Antarctica?
- What is the effect of differentiated instruction on elementary school children?

Assessment Opportunities

Formative Assessment—The formative assessment is completed during this game by visiting and listening to the teams as they work on finding their artifact. Some of the possible things that might show understanding: students looking up authors to see who they are and what they have done;

students talking about types of sources, such as whether they are peer-reviewed; discussions of how authors can be easier to look up in library databases compared to websites; and comments that different authors may have varied takes on the topic depending on their backgrounds.

Summative Assessment—The rubric in table 6.2 will be completed by the librarian and/or course instructor during the presentations. It provides an assessment of the understanding of authority shown by the students. It also contains some components that are just related to scoring the game. When filling out the rubric for each team, it is also important to consider the understanding that is shown by the questions asked. The questions may show a deeper understanding than the presentations.

Table 6.2
Rubric for scoring the game "Respect My Authority"

	Expert Learner	**Intermediate Learner**	**Novice Learner**
Clarifies how authority develops expertise.	Recognizes that an authority on the topic will possess years of experience and/or education and/or an extensive publication history.	Is able to explain how the author/creator had developed their expertise.	States author/creator was expert without further explanation as to how this was determined.
Clarifies authority within larger context.	Is able to articulate how this authority represents a specific thought within the larger topic by noting details such as differing opinions in the topic, new research, or prevailing discourses.	Will note that there are some differences in opinions on the topic.	Provides artifact as the isolated truth on a topic without consideration as to how it relates to other sources or authority.

Table 6.2

Rubric for scoring the game "Respect My Authority"

	Expert Learner	Intermediate Learner	Novice Learner
Clarifies how authority depends on context.	Articulates how the expertise held by the author/creator is important and fits within the context of the topic/research question.	Notes how authority depends on the context of the research topic but does not describe how the authority of their artifact matches the need of the current topic.	Shows no understanding that authority in one context does not mean authority is valid in another context.
Presentation flows, makes logical sense.	3	2	1
Presentation represents a combined group effort.	3	2	1
Questions are asked.	3	2	1

Notes/Modifications/Accommodations

If students are having trouble developing reasons why something is authoritative, you could use prompt questions such as these: What are the author's credentials? Has he or she written other things on this topic? Where did you find the artifact? Or how does where it is found affect the authority?

In order to encourage students to utilize a broad range of resources, this lesson may be best done after the students have some experience using different library databases. This should result in sources more varied than those that would be found by everyone conducting the same Google search and will allow for a broader discussion on the way in which authority is developed.

This game is effective in that it closely resembles the actual research process conducted by students. By opening up the search to all information resources, it is possible to see in detail the actual thinking done by students rather than limiting the requirement to use a specific library resource.

This game can be played by a wide range of students. The content of the question will differ depending on the course. It may be helpful to work with the course instructor to develop a question on a topic related to class discussion. More experienced researchers should offer more detailed analysis of what constitutes authority. Graduate-level classes may also initiate discussions on how ideas in the discipline have changed or on new research that is being conducted.

Due to the fact that a part of this game focuses on a presentation, it may be very appropriate to use it within a speech or oral communications course. This would be another way for the students to present in class, and it could provide the course instructor with an opportunity to grade the students. It may also be used as a practice exercise on how to organize and develop a persuasive argument. By connecting these features, the students will see the importance of a clear argument outside of the classroom. It may also help the development of stronger presentations by having the students view it as a structured talk rather than as a random ramble of thoughts. If the game is used in a speech class, it would be possible for the course instructor to judge the presentations using a different rubric focusing on communication criteria, while the librarian uses the summative rubric in table 10.2. These scores can then be combined in selecting the winning team.

Lesson Plan 3. Group Work
Lesson Plan Purpose

This lesson plan offers **practice in determining authority**. Students must judge the authority of various sources in order to determine the quality of information that is being presented. They must consider how the context of a question will affect the authority of those providing relevant information.

Learning Objective

Students will establish the authority of a resource in a specific context in order to determine reliable information on a topic.

Audience

Class size from 4 to 200. Undergraduates through graduate students.

Procedures

Time—15–20 minutes.

Supplies—Cards containing information about each student's persona during the group work. Preplanned information needs. Sheets for the students to record their final thoughts from the discussion (figure 6.1).

Process—Students are put into groups of 4–5.

INTRODUCTION—LIBRARIAN'S SCRIPT: *Today in your groups you will have a discussion, at the end of which you will develop a list of individuals with high authority, medium authority, and low authority. Each group will be given a stack of cards. There will be a persona card for each individual and an information need or question card. Everyone will choose a persona card. Then go around your group and introduce yourself using the persona that you chose. Then someone will read the information need or question card. You will then discuss the topic and your authority to talk about the topic. You will have ten minutes for your introductions and discussion. At the end of the discussion, your group will need to develop a list of individuals with high authority, medium authority, and low authority. For each individual, you will give the reasoning for the specific categorization. These sheets will be handed in at the end.*

EXAMPLE CARD GROUPINGS:
- Information Need/Question: What is the best way to stop a two-year-old from biting other people?

  Personas: Parent of three teenagers. Five-year-old child. Dentist. Psychology student. Family lifestyle blogger.
- Information Need/Question: What is the best way to handle stress?

  Personas: CEO of pharmaceutical company. Yoga instructor. Therapist. Life coach. High school counselor.
- Information Need/Question: What is the best method to protect a company's technology infrastructure?

Personas: Computer science professor. Member of the hacker group Anonymous. CIA operative. CEO of IBM. Head of a business IT department.

- Information Need/Question: What is the impact of Sylvia Plath upon current feminist theory?

Personas: Poet. PhD in British literature. Researcher with five articles published on Plath in the 1990s. Researcher with two articles published on Plath within the past five years. Plath's grandchild.

Individuals with high authority	How do you know?
• • •	
Individuals with medium authority	How do you know?
• • •	
Individuals with low authority	How do you know?
• • •	

FIGURE 6.1

Fact sheet for listing individuals with varying levels of authority

Assessment Opportunities

Formative Assessment—Formative assessment can be accomplished by meeting with the groups as they are filling out their fact sheets (figure 6.1). It is at this time that you can help guide their thinking and lead them to consider how their topic or research question affects the different types of authority, the bias of the authority, or the position of the authority within the larger topic.

Summative Assessment—The sheets (figure 6.1) filled out by the groups at the end of the discussion will provide the artifact to be used for the summative assessment. The rubric in table 6.3 provides example criteria with which to review the responses made by the students.

Table 6.3
Rubric for assessing fact sheets filled out by groups.

	Expert Learner	Intermediate Learner	Novice Learner
Recognizes different types of authority.	Describes the different types of methods available to gain expertise and notes how the specific methods are applicable within the specific context being discussed.	Articulates that expertise can be achieved due to a number of criteria such as education, experience, or employment.	Does not take into account that expertise may be acquired through a variety of means.
Positions authority within the larger context of topic.	Describes the authority within the larger context while referring to possible disputes within the topic and how the prevailing stance was developed.	Can articulate why certain authorities would hold a certain view or position on a topic due to their bias or privilege.	Recognizes authority may hold a bias on the topic.

Notes/Modifications/Accommodations

This lesson can be used with a range of students by modifying the information need or question and personas. For general classes, the questions can cover basic information needed by students both in class and in their lives. For classes within a specific discipline, the information and personas can be shifted to address both topics within the field and authorities that represent the types of resource sources they will be exposed to within the field. This acclimates them to the fact that there are specific types of "expert" sources within their field. For graduate students and those deeply involved in their disciplines, it would be possible to insert personas of specific individuals known within the field. These types of personas would allow the discussion to explore the concept that ideas within a field may change and that the prevailing theories may not always be accepted.

It is possible to give each group the same question and personas or to give each group a different question and personas. When using the same question and personas throughout the class, it would be possible to have a larger discussion at the end where the students could share their papers and be able to evaluate the reasoning of other groups. The variety offered by using different questions and personas allows for a greater range of discussion within the classroom.

Note

1. Association of College and Research Libraries, *Framework for Information Literacy for Higher Education* (Chicago: Association of College and Research Libraries, 2015), 4, http://www.ala.org/acrl/standards/ilframework.

Bibliography

Association of College and Research Libraries. *Framework for Information Literacy for Higher Education*. Chicago: Association of College and Research Libraries, 2015. http://www.ala.org/acrl/standards/ilframework.

CHAPTER 7

Framework Concept
Information Creation as a Process

Information in any format is produced to convey a message and is shared via a selected delivery method. The iterative processes of researching, creating, revising, and disseminating information vary, and the resulting product reflects these differences.[1]

Lesson Plan 1. Humor
Lesson Plan Purpose

This lesson plan offers an **introduction to the research process**. Students must work together to create and outline the steps they take when conducting research.

Learning Objective

Students will develop and analyze the creation of a research process in order explore how process affects the final information.

Audience

Undergraduate students. Class size from 5 to 30.

Procedures

Time—20 minutes

Supplies—Paper and pencil. Final questions for students to complete. These could be completed either with paper in class or electronically and sent to the librarian.

Process—

LIBRARIAN'S SCRIPT: *Today we are going to create step-by-step instructions on how to do research for a paper for someone who has never had to do research before. This means that it will be very important for us to list out each step and provide details that will be helpful. I am sure you have all been a part of a class where, when the professor says "we" are going to do something, it really means that there is one student who will really do it all. That will not be the case today, as we will all work together to create these instructions, and everyone will contribute. In order for that to happen, we are going to write our instructions one person at a time with everyone adding six words. We will just go around the room so everyone can share. We will also need to keep a record of our instructions so after you add your six words, you will need to write the next person's six words down on our sheet of instructions. I will start us off: "The first step in research is…" Now, who will go next while I write down your words?*

The instructions and paper and pencil continue around the room as each student adds six words. Every student should contribute at least once, with the final number of additions depending on the instructions that are created. After the instructions are completed, the librarian takes the sheet and thanks the students for their work.

To complete our step-by-step instructions, I would like you to answer the following two questions to be turned in: What steps, if any, do you think are missing from our instructions? How does following these steps affect the quality of the final research paper? I will now read our instructions to remind you of what we came up with. The answers will either be collected or e-mailed to the librarian.

Assessment Opportunities

Formative Assessment—The formative assessment is completed while the students are creating the instructions. It would be possible to see if they miss any major parts of the process. If necessary, you could let them know that they could add something else in the steps if wanted: "Before *xxx*, you will need to…"

Summative Assessment—The summative assessment will look at the answers to the two questions. These can be addressed using the rubric in table 7.1.

Table 7.1
Rubric for assessing students' answers to the two questions.

	Expert Learner	**Intermediate Learner**	**Novice Learner**
Understands the process to create information.	Notes a clear understanding of the steps involved in creating information including references to ideas such as using additional resources, placing the process within the larger field, and using a reiterative process of developing information.	Shows an understanding of the idea that there are unique processes to create information, but may overlook some steps.	Recognizes that there are steps to create information, but process provided relies on very basic steps. May believe that all information is created using the same process.
Understands that process affects quality and use of information.	Discusses how certain steps will affect quality and impact of the final information.	Notes how taking time with research means a quality product. Focus is on the information creator in isolation.	Limits comments to the process as simply requirements within an assignment.

Notes/Modifications/Accommodations

When providing the instructions for this lesson, the tone used by the instructor will provide the prompt for the students to understand that the work they will do to create the instructions will be fun. A lighthearted approach lets the students know that they are encouraged to enjoy themselves.

Humor may be found in any number of instances in this lesson: students counting words, attempts to finish sentences that others start, directions that take turns no one is expecting. Due to the fact that each student is responsible for adding only six words, there should not be undue stress on any individual who is having trouble thinking of the next thing to add. Also, as each student is asked to perform the same task, there should be a group unity developed.

It would be possible that instead of having the students write down the words of the next student, the instructor would type the words into a Word document that was being projected on a screen. This would allow everyone to see what has been said in order to get an overall understanding of the process as it is being developed. This does take away some of the group participation as the students are required only to talk.

This lesson could easily be modified to have the students create instructions for any number of information types. These could run a wide gamut from a Tweet to a memo to a book. For those in discipline-specific courses, it may be useful to have them consider how to write items that they will encounter either in their courses or once they enter their chosen field. Art majors may talk about how to write an artist statement. Chemistry majors may talk about how to write a lab report.

Another variation stemming from the idea of different information types is to split the class up into groups and assign each group a different type of information for which to create instructions. After all of the groups have developed their instructions, as a group the students would develop the connection between their information type and need. They would then share their instructions and need with the rest of the class. This option allows the class to see the different types of information available and consider how these types are developed in relation to what types of information needs they meet. Small-group work would be especially applicable in larger classes in order to ensure that everyone stays engaged. It would also be necessary for each student to provide more than six words in smaller groups.

Lesson Plan 2. Game
Lesson Plan Purpose

This lesson plan offers a **reinforcement of the process involved in conducting a research experiment, publishing the findings, and replicating the findings.** Students will complete a game followed by questions to analyze the process.

Learning Objective

Students will analyze aspects of a research study in order to describe the intricacies of the process and its resulting effect upon a field.

Audience

Mid- to upper-level undergraduate students and beginning graduate students in science fields. Class size from 3 to 50, with students split into groups of 3 to 5 to play the game.

Procedures

Time—15–20 minutes to play the game. 10–20 minutes for assessment.

Supplies—A deck of Research Study cards (figure 7.1) for each group of 3 to 5 players. A copy of the rules for each group. Each group will also need a table or flat surface to play the game on.

Process: Game Rules—

PURPOSE: To become a well-known researcher in your field by developing an accepted research theory. To do this you will need to collect characteristics of a reliable study, including an original idea, positive results, and acceptance by peer review. You will then prove your research theory through a series of replicated studies with positive results. The first person with a complete study and three positive replicated studies wins.

GAME PLAY:

1. The dealer shuffles the cards and deals out five to each player. The remaining cards are placed facedown in a stack in the middle of the playing surface.

2. The player on the dealer's left starts by drawing the top card. The player is trying to make a set of the three Research Study cards (Original

Idea, Positive Results, Peer Review). If a set is made, the cards are set down faceup in front of the player. At the end of each player's turn, he or she takes a card from the cards in hand and places it faceup in a discard pile.

3. Play continues clockwise, with the next player drawing a card either from the discard pile or the deck. Players can pick up as many cards as needed from the withdraw pile, adding them to their individual hand. Each player attempts to create a set of Research Study cards. At the end of each player's turn, he or she again takes a card from the cards in hand and adds it to the top of the withdraw pile.

4. Once a Research Study set has been completed, the player needs to play three Replicated Study (Positive) cards. Only one Replicated Study (Positive) card can be played per turn.

5. Once a player has a Research Study set, other players can play a Replicated Study (Negative) card faceup in front of another player's Research Study. If a player gets a Replicated Study (Negative) card from another player, their next turn is forfeited. After losing a turn, the student will turn the Replicated Study (Negative) card facedown. Three Replicated Study (Negative) cards will invalidate a Research Study, and the owner of that study cannot win with that Research Study. That player will continue in the game and can play Replicated Study (Negative) cards on other players' Research Studies.

6. The first person who has played a complete set of the three Research Study cards and three Replicated Study (Positive) cards wins.

Each turn, after drawing a card or cards, the player can place down three cards forming a matched Research Study, place one Replicated Study (Positive) card on his or her own study, or place one Replicated Study (Negative) card on an opponent's study.

After the game is finished, the students should be given as a group the following questions to be discussed and answered. In order to promote participation by every group member, ask that each person write the answer to one of the questions. Note that the different handwriting for each question will let you know that they have all participated.

- In order to win the game and get a complete research theory, you had to have three positive replicated studies. What are the point of these studies in the real world?

- What do you think happens to real research studies when someone repeats the study and finds different results?

- The game required that you collect an original idea, positive result, and acceptance by peer review in order to make a complete research study. What else can you think of that is necessary to complete a research study?
- The research study set you made had positive results. Is there ever a time when it would be appropriate to publish negative results?
- The creation of a research theory produced in this manner creates very specific information. What would this type of information be used for? Consider who would use it and what type of questions they would answer.

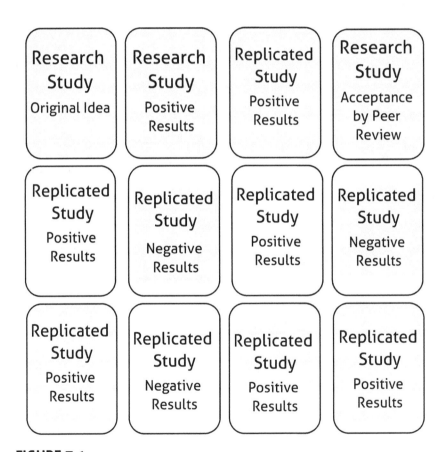

FIGURE 7.1

Research Study cards

Assessment Opportunities

Formative Assessment—Formative assessment for this lesson can be done while the students are filling out the questions in their groups. The groups may ask for assistance or clarification of individual questions, which allows you to gauge their understanding. If the groups are not asking questions, one structured way to do a formative assessment is to listen to each group as they complete one question. By taking time to listen to the entire thought process and discussion of the group, you will be able to get a clearer picture of their understanding. Did they know what to write about right away, or did they have to work through an answer? When listening to one group for an extended period, it is important to stay as unobtrusive as possible. The students should work through the questions on their own as much as possible rather than turning to the librarian to provide them with answers.

Summative Assessment—The answers to the questions completed by the students will allow for the summative assessment. The rubric in table 7.2 provides criteria corresponding to the various questions.

Table 7.2 Rubric for assessing responses to questions following the "Research Study" game			
	Expert Learner	**Intermediate Learner**	**Novice Learner**
Replicated studies (Questions 1–2)	Details how wide acceptance on a topic takes the agreement and approval of a number of professionals within a field. Notes how it is more than a simple number of studies to prove something, but also the quality of those studies.	May note how new ideas need to fit into what is already accepted in a discipline, so it takes multiple research to prove.	Provides the basic idea that if something happens or is done a number of times it must be true.

Process to create information (Question 3)	Notes a clear understanding of the steps involved in creating information type, including references to ideas such as using additional resources, placing the process within the larger field, and using the reiterative process of developing information.	Shows an understanding of the idea that there are unique processes to create information, but may overlook some steps.	Recognizes that there are steps to create information, but process provided relies on very basic steps. May believe that all information is created using the same process.
Negative information (Question 4)	Comments on how there is often a bias shown within published research that favors positive results and how such a system cuts out research that may help advance the field.	Notes that negative results could be published, but without providing discussion as to why.	Notes that only positive results should be published.
Use of information (Question 5)	Discusses how the standard method of communication within a field allows its members to communicate effectively and approach problems in a manner that is accepted by all and allows for comparison and evaluation of new ideas.	Discusses how the process of information creation has been accepted as standard by members of a professional field and as such provides the field with a set way to communicate.	Limits comments to how research is used by professionals. No discussion as to why it is used.

Notes/Modifications/Accommodations

The structure of this game using replicated studies is probably best suited for students in the sciences rather than the humanities, as it more closely resembles the research within that field. The students should already have a general understanding of the publication process. Having the course faculty member discuss the publication process, perhaps using his or her own work as an example, within a specific field would be helpful as it provides context for the students and an experience to draw from. This game is a way to have students work from a basic understanding in order to engage with the content and consider it in more depth.

To add some additional interest and discussion points, an additional card could be added to the deck—Research Study (Accepted by predatory journal). This card would allow the player to skip over the step of collecting the three Research Study cards, but would require six Replicated Study (Positive) cards to win the game. This would be a way to introduce the idea of predatory journals and addresses the idea that when choosing where to publish a work an author must make conscious decisions in regard to where he or she will submit and how that placement will affect the impact of the work as well as how others view it. It also encourages the students to consider the difference between a short-term gain and a longer-term goal.

This game is set up to require some evaluation and strategy on the part of the students in order to make it more interesting and engaging. For example, the students must consider whether it would be better to play a Negative card to stall another player's collection or to play a Positive card on their own collections. However, it is also meant to be easy enough for the students to have an opportunity to think about the publishing process as they are playing.

The questions asked can be edited, added to, or subtracted from as necessary. For classes within a specific discipline, it may be appropriate to edit the questions to focus more specifically on how research in that particular field is conducted. For example, there may be a question that places the research theory within a conference setting or that notes the importance of collaborators in developing an idea. Some of the questions (e.g., number 4) encourage the students to consider the creation process from a different perspective by looking not only at actual steps in the process, but also at how different information is treated within that process.

Lesson Plan 3. Group Work

Lesson Plan Purpose

This lesson plan offers **reinforcement to the process of creating information**. Students will connect ideas, process steps, and use different types of resources in the process of creating a concept map that shows their understanding of the connection between these items.

Learning Objective

Students will develop a conceptual structure in order to show understanding of the processes involved in creating information.

Audience

Undergraduates or graduate students. Class size from 5 to 200.

Procedures

Time—15–20 minutes

Supplies—Blank paper for creating concept map. Starter list of topics for concept map. Example concept maps (figures 7.2 and 7.3).

Process—After a discussion in class on how information is created through a process, students are divided into groups of 4–5. They are instructed to utilize what they have learned along with what they already know in order to create a concept map. Let them know that a concept map is a visual representation of how different ideas and concepts connect. A concept map should be made understandable to others by the inclusion of connecting lines and phrases. Providing a variety of sample concept maps (see figures 7.2 and 7.3) will probably also be helpful to give them some ideas on the different ways they would be able to create their maps. Sample concept maps also can be found online. A variety of web and flow charts would be applicable to the concept maps they will be creating. These samples should focus on the broad topic of how to create a concept map rather than offering examples of the specific concept maps they will be creating.

Let the students know that the words they are being given are just a start to what they can do with their concept map. There is no limit to what they can add to their map. They will be given a stack of topics that can be included in their concept map. The stack of words is to be divided evenly between all group members. They will then begin with one person laying down a word. Each person will be responsible for adding their words to the concept map. As each student adds a word, he or she will need to explain the reason for where it is being placed and how it connects to the other words. Students can also add additional words before they finish with the supplied words. After the words are all laid out, the group has the option to move already-placed words and add new words in order to create a more complete map. Once the students are comfortable with their concept map, they will need to transfer it to the piece of paper. This will be handed in to the librarian.

Some example suggested words for the concept map:

- magazine
- newspaper
- blog
- reporter
- professional
- editor
- reviewer
- research
- revision
- discussion
- citation
- fact check
- draft
- study
- author
- experiment
- how-to
- edit
- topic
- interview
- expert
- general population

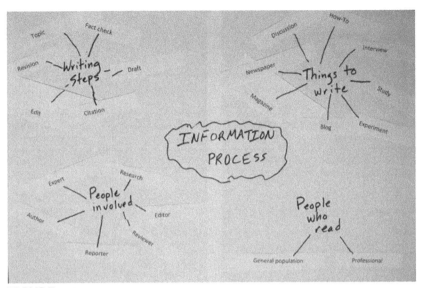

FIGURE 7.2

Sample concept map

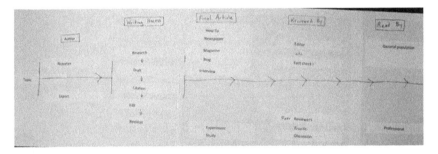

FIGURE 7.3

Sample concept map

Assessment Opportunities

Formative Assessment—The formative assessment is accomplished while the students are working in groups. As each student is adding a word it is possible to assess his or her understanding of the relationship between the different concepts. Then during the final review and possible rearrangement of the concept map, it is possible to hear questions that the group members still have on how the words can go together. The students should be able to answer many of each other's questions.

Summative Assessment—The summative assessment will be done by analyzing the concept maps handed in by the groups. The rubric in table 7.3 could be used for the assessment.

Table 7.3 Rubric for assessing concept maps			
	Expert Learner	**Intermediate Learner**	**Novice Learner**
Understands the process to create information.	Notes a clear understanding of the steps involved in creating information type, including references to ideas such as using additional resources, placing the process within the larger field, and using a reiterative process of developing information.	Shows an understanding of the idea that there are unique processes to create information, but may overlook some steps.	Recognizes that there are steps to create information, but process provided relies on very basic steps. May believe that all information is created using the same process.

Notes/Modifications/Accommodations

One method to promote increased engagement with the content would be to provide the list of keywords and topics to the students before the class and have them bring in a draft concept map to class. This could help them to start thinking about the concept. Then during the lesson, the librarian could lead a full class discussion on some of the different processes that are completed when information is produced. After this discussion, the students would then be divided into their groups, where they would compare their concept maps and add any additional information that they may have gathered during the full class discussion. It would also be possible to cut out the full class discussion and just have the groups talk about their individual concept maps in order to develop a final concept map together. This option does allow for a greater number of students to talk, as there can be several discussions occurring at once as opposed to just one single discussion. This means the students will engage with the content at least twice as they create their own concept map and then join with a group to create another. When collecting the final concept maps, it would be helpful to have the individual maps attached to the final map in order to compare how the concept maps have changed.

While this lesson is designed to follow a discussion of how information goes through different processes in order to be created, it could also be set up to allow the student groups to just get together in order to create their concept maps. They will be able to share their individual knowledge within their groups and work together to create understanding.

By splitting up the cards among the group members, you are making sure that they all participate and engage in the group work. This allows everyone to make connections and contribute. By requiring the students to participate in the beginning of the group work, it is more likely that they will continue to engage with the material as the lesson continues.

The stock words given to the students can be modified depending on the class. Graduate classes may focus on information produced for peer-reviewed journals, conferences, or white papers. Classes within a specific discipline may consider information that is common within that specific field. In order to create a concept map that is sufficiently robust, it may be a good idea to provide each student with at least four to five stock words to start, and to which they can add additional words.

Note

1. Association of College and Research Libraries, *Framework for Information Literacy for Higher Education* (Chicago: Association of College and Research Libraries, 2015), 5, http://www.ala.org/acrl/standards/ilframework.

Bibliography

Association of College and Research Libraries. *Framework for Information Literacy for Higher Education*. Chicago: Association of College and Research Libraries, 2015. http://www.ala.org/acrl/standards/ilframework.

CHAPTER 8

Framework Concept
Information Has Value

Information possesses several dimensions of value, including as a commodity, as a means of education, as a means to influence, and as a means of negotiating and understanding the world. Legal and socioeconomic interests influence information production and dissemination.[1]

Lesson Plan 1. Humor
Lesson Plan Purpose

This lesson plan **introduces the concept of plagiarism**. Students will look at a specific instance of plagiarism within an unusual context in order to initiate discussion on how plagiarism affects individuals in a range of circumstances.

Learning Objective

Students will explore a specific plagiarism example in order to discuss the impact of plagiarism upon different individuals.

117

Audience

Lower-level undergraduate students. Class size 5 to 200.

Procedures

Time—15–25 minutes

Supplies—A copy of *Shadow Bear* and the original article it plagiarizes. Projector and screen. Paper for minute paper replies.

Process—This lesson deals with plagiarism by using the example of the romance novel *Shadow Bear* by Cassie Edwards. Edwards plagiarized the article "Toughing It Out in the Badlands" by Paul Tolme from the summer 2005 issue of *Defenders Magazine*. The unlikely juxtaposition of finding an environmental article used as dialogue in a romance novel provides the structure for the humor.

LIBRARIAN'S SCRIPT: *Today we are going to have a story time. Sit back as we travel to 1850 to hear the story of a young pioneer woman and a Lakota chief. Theirs was a forbidden love filled with interesting dialogue.* (Proceed to read the plagiarized section from the book starting at the beginning of chapter 22.) *Well, I have now learned something about black-footed ferrets. Something I was not quite expecting in choosing this book. Did anyone find this section of the book a little off? Why? Perhaps you would be interested in reading part of this article published online in* Defenders Magazine.

Project the section of the article containing the plagiarized text. It may also be interesting to tell the students that to professors reading a paper, plagiarized text often sounds just as out of place as the dialogue in the book.

Notice anything similar? What is happening in this situation? What do you think should happen to the author? Have you ever heard about plagiarism happening outside of school? What if the roles had been reversed and the magazine article plagiarized a romance novel? The author said after this was discovered that she did not know she was supposed to cite source material. What do you think about this statement?

After the discussion, the students can complete a minute paper to wind up the lesson: "What are the effects on the original author when someone plagiarizes his or her work?"

Assessment Opportunities

Formative Assessment—The formative assessment takes place during the discussion of the book. In answering the questions and discussing the issue, the students should talk about topics such as how the author was trying to make money in selling her book and how plagiarism results in different outcomes depending on the situation.

Summative Assessment—The summative assessment will be done by evaluating the responses to the minute paper. The rubric in table 8.1 provides criteria to apply to the papers.

Table 8.1 Rubric for evaluating minute papers			
	Expert Learner	**Intermediate Learner**	**Novice Learner**
Value of intellectual property.	Discusses several dimensions of value that may be lost by the author including monetary, reputation, and intellectual property. Specifically notes how value is determined by situation and type of information produced.	Notes that authors may lose out on several different types of value, but offers no discussion on what the values mean or how they differ depending on the type of information.	Basic response just discusses one value of information such as monetary gain.

Notes/Modifications/Accommodations

Paul Tolme wrote a response to this situation that was published online by *Newsweek* on January 14, 2008. It provides excerpts from the book and the article.[2] This article would provide enough information for the lesson. Within a more flipped classroom, it may be interesting to have students read the article beforehand and then have the discussion in class.

This example differs from many of the lectures students hear about plagiarism. Often plagiarism is considered only within academia. It is important for students to understand that information has value and that the misuse of intellectual property is an issue that will extend beyond their time in college. Fair use and copyright issues will continue to be a part of their lives whether they are putting out content on social media or writing something for their jobs.

Other real-life examples of plagiarism could also be used in place of the book example provided. There are a number of instances in which reporters plagiarize other published works, or public officials plagiarize within speeches. These also provide real-life examples to start a discussion.

This lesson can be the introduction to a number of different topics. It could simply lead into a discussion of different types of plagiarism and how to correctly cite sources. It could also lead to discussions on fair use, copyright, and public domain.

Lesson Plan 2. Game
Lesson Plan Purpose

This lesson plan offers an introduction to the **value of knowledge** within a specific context. Students will assign worth to knowledge and supplies in order to reach a goal. They will then discuss their thoughts on how worth is assigned to knowledge both within the specific context of the game and in the outside world.

Learning Objective

Students will develop and discuss different systems of obtaining information in order to gain understanding on how information possesses varying degrees of value.

Audience

Lower-level undergraduates to graduate students. Class size from 10 to 30.

Procedures

Time—40–60 minutes

Supplies—Premade cards listing supplies and knowledge. Cards should be color-coded (blue for supplies, yellow for knowledge) with blank additional cards provided for each student in the color of the knowledge cards.

Process: Game Rules—

PURPOSE: To gather supplies and knowledge in order to survive on the deserted island.

SET-UP—LIBRARIAN'S SCRIPT: *You and the rest of your classmates were on a plane flying across the ocean. Suddenly the plane lurches and the pilot comes over the intercom telling you that one of the engines has just shut down and they will be attempting to make an emergency landing. Over the sound of the plane and the shouts of the passengers, you try to listen to the flight attendant and review the emergency procedures. The plane starts a steep dive and you hold onto your armrests. You see a spot of green and tan below amid a wide expanse of blue. The pilot is attempting to land on an island, and you brace yourself for a crash landing. After everything has stopped moving, you discover the plane has come to a stop next to some trees on the edge of a wide beach. The plane will never be able to fly again but remains almost intact except for the communication system. All of your fellow passengers are alive with just bumps and bruises. As you start to get out of your seat and exit the plane, you see the under-plane storage has been torn open, and there is a mad rush to get the bags and materials they contain. Everyone is trying to get supplies to help them survive, as there is no telling when rescue will come.*

You will need to get individual supplies and knowledge for your time on the island. Your task is to gather what you think you will need in order to survive. You can use whatever means you choose to work with or against your fellow passengers. There are two types of cards you will get. The blue cards are supplies. These are static items that can be used. The yellow cards are knowledge. Knowledge is something that multiplies. If you possess a knowledge card, you can write that knowledge on a blank yellow card and give it to someone else while keeping your original card.

To help you figure out what you need to survive, here are some facts about the island: temperatures range from fifty-five to ninety degrees; it contains a mix of trees and open beach; there are small birds, mammals, and reptiles living on the island; there is a stream with fresh water; and the island is about five miles across.

Hand out the cards, or have the cards spread out on a table facedown for the students to choose. *For the next fifteen minutes, you need to interact with your fellow passengers and gather what you need to survive. After that time, you will share how long you think you will live, and we will discuss what happened during the game.*

After the students have spent the 15 minutes gathering materials, have them sit down and consider their supplies and knowledge. Ask those who think they will survive a day to stand up, then have those who think they will survive a week to stand up, then two weeks, a month, two months, and so on. Each time fewer individuals will stand up. When there is only one person standing, you can declare this person the winner. After the winner is declared, it is time to start the discussion. The question prompts start by considering the game and then moving into the value of knowledge and information. If the students are having trouble starting the conversation, ask the winner to start the discussion.

QUESTION PROMPTS: How did you get supplies and knowledge? Trade? Free exchange? Were any partnerships formed? Did you just pool all your resources? How did you decide how much supplies were worth? Did you consider short-term versus long-term goals when getting supplies and knowledge? Was there a difference in the worth between supplies and knowledge? Did anyone trade or sell knowledge that they had gotten from someone else?

At the end of the discussion, provide the students with a minute paper prompt to complete before they leave the classroom: "What did this game make you realize about the value of knowledge?"

SAMPLE SUPPLIES:

- a four-person tent
- a lighter
- a pocketknife
- a suitcase of sweaters
- a duffle bag with $10,000 cash
- shampoo and sunscreen
- prescription pain pills and aspirin
- yarn and knitting needles
- stuffed animals
- a rifle
- twenty bullets
- a book on poisonous insects
- fishing pole

SAMPLE KNOWLEDGE:

- how to build a bridge
- how to build a fire
- how to pick edible plants

- how to skin an animal
- how to tie knots

Assessment Opportunities

Formative Assessment—The formative assessment will take place during the discussion after the game. Students will be able to demonstrate an understanding that knowledge has an innate value and that different knowledge will be worth more or less depending on the situation. They may also discuss how they would want to keep knowledge to themselves in some situations or how they may try to enhance the usefulness of their knowledge in order to get something else.

Summative Assessment—The summative assessment will take place through a review of the minute paper responding to the prompt. The rubric in table 8.2 gives some criteria for evaluating the minute paper.

Table 8.2 Rubric for evaluating the minute paper			
	Expert Learner	**Intermediate Learner**	**Novice Learner**
Value of Information	Discusses how various types of information possess different values depending on the situation. Can provide examples on the different types of value such as monetary or intellectual property.	Recognizes that obtaining information requires effort on the part of an individual and therefore the resulting knowledge has value.	Notes the basic idea that some information has value when it is rare and has instant application.

Notes/Modifications/Accommodations

The minute paper prompt provided is meant to be very open-ended in order to elicit a range of responses from the students on their ideas about value and information. It is possible to create a more focused prompt to encourage students to think about a specific issue, perhaps within their discipline or in relation to something that is occurring in the news.

The discussion after the game could be steered in a variety of directions. A focus on free exchange of knowledge and partnerships could lead into open-access publishing. Discussion on the idea of others selling your knowledge could lead to plagiarism. The idea of forming partnerships could lead to research communities and different schools of thought within a discipline. The concept of trying to get something for knowledge that is not that useful could lead to the topic of publishing insignificant articles within a field in order to reach promotion or tenure goals.

Lesson Plan 3. Group Work
Lesson Plan Purpose

This lesson plan offers an introduction to **how companies can use personal information for monetary gain**. Students will focus on advertisements within their personal social media accounts in order to discuss how companies are using their personal information and search history.

Learning Objective

Students will analyze targeted advertisements in order to explore how their personal information is being monetized.

Audience

Lower- to upper-level undergraduate students. Class size from 12 to 200.

Procedures

Time—15–20 minutes

Supplies—Internet access for students. Worksheet for each group to complete (figure 8.1).

Process—Students should be divided into groups of 4. Have each group number off from 1 to 4. When each person has a number, they should be given details about each specific role. Member 1 will be the Keeper. The responsibilities of this member are to keep track of the time to ensure the worksheet is completed and to keep everyone on track in case the conversation starts to stray from the topic. Member 2 will be the Recorder. The responsibility of this member is to record the team's answers on the worksheet. Member 3 and member 4 will be the Case Studies. The responsibilities of these members

Group member names:

Keeper –

Recorder –

Case Study One –

Case Study Two –

Directions:

Case Study One and Case Study Two group members, go to your Facebook accounts. Look for the first three ads on your page. These could be the advertisements on the right side of the page or Sponsored Posts within your newsfeed. Fill out the following chart using these ads.

	What is the ad for?	**Why is this ad showing up? Is there a Facebook like or personal characteristic to which it refers?**	**Have you seen this ad before?**
Example	KnitPicks – yarn company	I like several Facebook pages on knitting	Yes, it comes up frequently.
Case Study One—Ad 1			
Case Study One—Ad 2			
Case Study One—Ad 3			
Case Study Two—Ad 1			
Case Study Two—Ad 2			
Case Study Two—Ad 3			

FIGURE 8.1

Worksheet

are to open their Facebook accounts and find advertisements. They will also provide details about themselves as necessary to explain the advertisements. In addition to their specific responsibilities, each group member is required to take part in the discussion and offer experiences and thoughts in forming answers to the worksheet questions. If member 3 or 4 does not have a Facebook account, they can switch roles with another group member.

The worksheet will then be handed out. After each group has been given the worksheet, go through the directions and ask for questions. It may be helpful to provide a sample either orally or on the worksheet itself. When the groups understand the activity, they can begin their work. At the end of the time allotted, they will be asked to hand in their completed group worksheets. Having the directions on the worksheet as well as explained orally is helpful, as students may need to refer to what they need to do throughout the lesson.

The following questions should be answered by all group members. They refer to all advertisements that you see online, not just those on the Facebook pages of group members three and four. It is best to discuss each question first before recording an answer.

1. What advertisements do you see when you are browsing the Internet?

2. Do you notice when ads are targeted or show items that you have looked at previously?

3. Do you do anything to restrict how your information is used?

4. Do you know which companies are selling your information (search history, likes, etc.) or using your information to target ads?

5. How do you feel about targeted ads?

6. Should companies be able to sell your information (search history, likes, etc.) to other groups?

Assessment Opportunities

Formative Assessment—The formative assessment is accomplished while the students are completing the worksheets. It is during this time that the librarian can hear what students know about companies using their information for advertisements and prompt their discussions to how information including personal data has value.

Summative Assessment—Summative assessment will analyze the worksheets completed by the students. The rubric in table 8.3 provides structure on how to review the group's' work.

Table 8.3
Rubric for evaluating the worksheets

	Expert Learner	**Intermediate Learner**	**Novice Learner**
Commodification of personal data	Discusses the benefits and negatives within the structure of companies selling personal data. Notes how individual decisions responding to the system must be considered carefully.	Provides a one-sided stance on the use of personal data for advertising. This opinion could be either positive or negative.	Shows no understanding that personal data is being mined for commercial gain.

Notes/Modifications/Accommodations

This lesson works in very large classes, as it provides a greater number of students the chance to actively participate and discuss the content. In smaller classes, it may be possible to have a full class discussion at the end for groups to share any specific insights or ideas. Personal stories related to targeted advertisements may also be shared in order to explore the topic in more depth.

Even in situations in which individual students do not have a Facebook account, this lesson should still be applicable in that it is likely that there are enough students who do have accounts. This lesson also provides more flexibility, in that all students do not need to have access to a computer. Tablet or smartphone access will also provide students access to their Facebook accounts.

For some students, this lesson may prove to be eye-opening in regard to how companies use their information to make money and sell ads. As more ads appear online, individuals have a tendency to just overlook them or ignore their presence. Taking the time to look for these ads and consider why they are appearing makes students see the connection between all of their online activity. For example, Facebook may present an ad for the shirt that the student had been considering purchasing earlier in the day, or a hotel in the city for which they had purchased plane tickets. The fact that their online activity is being monitored and that companies are using this information to make money should make them consider how this could affect them in the future.

Notes

1. Association of College and Research Libraries, *Framework for Information Literacy for Higher Education* (Chicago: Association of College and Research Libraries, 2015), 6, http://www.ala.org/acrl/standards/ilframework.
2. Paul Tolme, "Move Over, 'Meerkat Manor,'" *Newsweek*, January 14, 2008, http://www.newsweek.com/move-over-meerkat-manor-87497.

Bibliography

Association of College and Research Libraries. *Framework for Information Literacy for Higher Education*. Chicago: Association of College and Research Libraries, 2015. http://www.ala.org/acrl/standards/ilframework.

Tolme, Paul. "Move Over, 'Meerkat Manor.'" *Newsweek*, January 14, 2008. http://www.newsweek.com/move-over-meerkat-manor-87497.

CHAPTER 9

Framework Concept
Research as Inquiry

Research is iterative and depends upon asking increasingly complex or new questions whose answers in turn develop additional questions or lines of inquiry in any field.[1]

Lesson Plan 1. Humor
Lesson Plan Purpose

This lesson plan offers an **introduction to the process of creating a research question**. Students will consider how a phenomenon can provoke a question that starts the research process.

Learning Objective

Students will understand that research starts with a question in order to begin their individual research process.

Audience

Students just learning about research. Basic undergraduate classes. Class size from 2 to 250.

Procedures

Time—20–30 minutes

Supplies—Ability to show video (projector with computer connection and screen). Video links cued and ready to play. Link to research article. Whiteboard.

Process—Introduce the section by noting that today we are going to discuss how research starts out as a question. Start by showing a clip or series of clips of individuals slipping on banana peels. Start the discussion by asking the students what questions they have after watching a video of someone falling on a banana peel. Write these questions on the whiteboard. These questions can be about the banana peels, pain, or any other topic. This is a time to allow the students to brainstorm and be creative. It also starts them thinking about and practicing developing questions that will help them as they later develop their own research questions. This helps prime their thinking for later application.

After developing a list of questions, comment that now that we have some preliminary questions, it is time to gather some basic data. Ask if anyone has slipped on a banana peel or known someone who has. Wait for a reply. This is an experiment that many people seem to have performed as children, especially on siblings. So given the data that we have and all the cultural references, is this a topic we want to consider in more depth?

When the class agrees, let them know that unfortunately someone has already done research on this topic. Show them the article "Frictional Coefficient under Banana Skin" by Kiyoshi Mabuchi, Kensei Tanaka, Daichi Uchijima, and Rina Sakai (*Tribology Online* 7, no. 3, Hiroshima 2011 Special Issue, Part I [2012]: 147–51, doi:10.2474/trol.7.147). Explain how this peer-reviewed research was given an Ig Nobel award. Share with students the idea of the Ig Nobel, which rewards research that has been done that seems improbable or silly but makes one think. You can then show the clip of the award being given for the banana peel research from the Ig Nobel YouTube Channel at https://youtu.be/LfpbEjs5umk.

End this lesson with a discussion on how research really starts with a question. There is something that you want to know, and research is how you work toward answering that question. The question is really the most important part, and figuring out a proper question will affect the ensuing research.

Assessment Opportunities

Formative Assessment—This lesson provides a built-in formative assessment when the students are asked to develop questions on the topic. Their ability or inability to create such a question will provide you with information on their understanding of how to create a research question. Beginning students will likely need more guidance on how to create a question.

Summative Assessment—One possible summative assessment would require collaboration with the course faculty. This lesson would likely be offered for a class that was about to develop a research question in order to conduct research resulting in a paper, speech, or project of some type. After the assignment was handed in, the research question posed could be assessed. If the assignment is evaluated by a rubric, it may be possible that the faculty member already has criteria for evaluating the research question or thesis statement. This is a common component for some rubrics. If not, the rubric in table 9.1 could be applied by the faculty member or librarian. This in-depth assessment is applicable to the final research question.

Table 9.1
Rubric for evaluating research question

	Expert Learner	**Intermediate Learner**	**Novice Learner**
Scope of question	Question focuses clearly on an issue within the topic that can be adequately addressed within the requirements of the paper/ project.	Question provides for some focus, showing a cursory rather than deep understanding of the topic.	Question is too broad for the required paper/ project showing a lack of understanding of the topic.
Complexity of question	Question requires complex compilation of data or insight from possibly varied disciplines.	Question requires some compilation of data or insight beyond facts.	Question requires simple gathering of facts and knowledge to answer.

Notes/Modifications/Accommodations

There are a large number of Ig Nobel prizes that could be used as an example to highlight the idea that research starts out as a question. If the class is within a discipline, it may be more interesting to discuss the prize as it relates to that field. The banana peel example was chosen above as it is a classic comic gag that will be well known to students. It also provides humor on a number of levels. First, there are those who enjoy physical humor and consider the simple act of someone falling to be funny. For those who do not enjoy physical humor, the example shows how it is possible to take something that seems childish and, by looking at it in another way, turn it into something insightful.

As a possible extension of this lesson that would allow for additional creative and critical thinking by the students, have the class go to the Ig Nobel prize page (http://www.improbable.com) to look at other research that has been done. As the site notes, it presents research that first makes you laugh and then makes you think. Have the students review the research and provide an example of how these findings could be applied to other situations or how this research will encourage new ideas. As an example, using the banana peel research above, application of the results could result in the development of a new natural lubricant. This assignment helps develop the idea that research is never completed, but rather provides the impetus for additional research and study.

While this lesson is labeled for an audience of undergraduates, the Ig Nobel site would also be a great place to start a discussion with graduate students. The topic with graduate students could focus on how to find a research question that has not been asked in their field by looking at previous research and finding gaps. The humor on the Ig Nobel site and the humor during the ceremonies is also geared toward those with more of an understanding of academia, which may appeal to graduate students more than to undergraduates.

Lesson Plan 2. Game
Lesson Plan Purpose

This lesson plan offers a **reinforcement of the process of creating a research question**. Students will put together an increasing number of ideas and facts to create a research question. They will end by responding to a prompt on research questions and by creating a preliminary question for their research.

Learning Objective

Students will create logical connections between different topics and facts in order to develop increasingly complex research questions.

Audience

Varied. Versions of this game can be used with any group of students from freshmen up to graduate students. Class size from 2 to 200. The game can be played in groups of up to 8 individuals. Larger classes will have more groups.

Procedures

Time—25–40 minutes

Supplies—Cards with ideas and facts. One set for each group of students up to 8. (Timers to limit length of turns.)

Process: Game Rules: "Always Questioning"—

PURPOSE: To collect idea and fact cards. After all the cards have been used, the person with the most cards is the winner.

GAME PLAY—INTRODUCTION—LIBRARIAN'S SCRIPT: *This game tests your creativity and ability to combine seemingly unrelated ideas and facts by creating increasingly detailed research questions. When developing a research question, the researcher, whether a professional or a student, must take ideas and facts and combine them in a way to discover something new. You will take on the role of a researcher today trying to develop a research question using various ideas and facts.*

1. Shuffle the deck of cards and lay them facedown in a pile in the center of the table.

2. The first player picks up the top card. After reading the fact or idea on the card, the player develops a research question related to that card. After the first player successfully develops a research question, the card is passed to the player on the left.

3. The player who just received the card must draw the top card from the pile. The player then develops a research question combining the idea or fact on the card drawn with the original card. This research question can build upon the research question originally developed or be completely original. After the second player develops a research question, both cards are passed to the next player on the left.

4. Play continues in this way, with each player including an additional fact or idea to the research question.

5. If a player cannot develop a research question using all of the ideas and facts, the cards must be handed back to the previous player. That player keeps these cards to be tallied at the end of the game. The player who could not develop a research question starts a new round by drawing a card and developing a research question using the new card.

6. Play continues until all of the cards have been drawn. Any cards still in play for an active research question are thrown out when there are no cards left.

7. Each player counts the number of fact or idea cards that have been collected. The one with the most cards wins.

EXAMPLE: There are five students playing. Abby starts by picking the fact card "Water is a liquid." She proposes the research question "How long does it take for a smartphone to be permanently damaged when submerged in liquid water?" Abby hands the card to Burt on her left, who picks up the idea card "Pet hair has practical uses." He creates the research question "Can pet hair be used as a buffer to help protect smartphones when submerged in liquid water?" (This research question builds upon the one prior.) Burt hands both cards to Carl, the player on his left. Carl draws the fact card "Coffee comes from beans." He offers the research question "Does dry roasting coffee beans to remove the liquid water from them over a fire made of pet hair change the flavor of the resulting brewed coffee?" (This research question does not build upon prior questions.) Carl then hands three cards to Dory, the player on his left. Dory draws the fact card "Peanuts are not actually nuts; they are legumes." She cannot think of a research question, so she hands the three cards back to Carl, who gets to keep them. She then comes up with a research question using the card she drew, "What are the characteristics that are needed to classify something as a nut?" She then hands the card to Eleanor, the player on her left.

After the games have been completed, debrief the students by having them write in a one-minute paper what they learned about research questions during the game. After noting what they have learned, have them include a preliminary research question for an upcoming paper or project.

Assessment Opportunities

Formative Assessment—Formative assessment can be accomplished during this lesson by listening to the research questions developed by the students during the game. While creating research questions with a number of facts and ideas will be difficult, it is more important to ensure that the students are able to develop a question from a single or two cards. By listening to the manner in which students combine the various facts and ideas, it is also possible to get some insight into their ability to organize information and connect it in meaningful ways. The structure of the game is developed so that each player is required to come up with a research question during their individual turns. This provides the opportunity for everyone to participate and practice developing a research question.

Summative Assessment—The summative assessment is accomplished using the one-minute paper handed in by the students. The rubric in table 9.2 offers suggested criteria to consider. The research question is not assessed to the extent expected in a final research paper or project due to the fact that it is only a preliminary research question, which could still be changed by the student.

Table 9.2
Rubric for evaluating minute papers

	Expert Learner	Intermediate Learner	Novice Learner
Development of research questions	Is able to describe how research questions can be developed by expanding the work of others or by developing original ideas of study.	May note the differences between coming up with a new question or using part of someone else's idea, but does not connect this to research done outside of class.	Offers little to no notice to the fact that research questions can be developed using different methods.

Table 9.2
Rubric for evaluating minute papers

	Expert Learner	**Intermediate Learner**	**Novice Learner**
Connection of different and unique ideas	Is able to talk about how research is often on the edge of a topic and pushes forward or combines with different fields to answer new questions.	Notes how connecting different facts and ideas creates interesting new questions.	May simply note that putting together different facts and ideas is difficult without any discussion of why that would be the case.
Preliminary research question	Combines various concepts to examine a gap or conflict within the topic.	Combines various concepts within the field to look at a topic that may already be known.	Focuses upon one issue within the topic. This issue may be too broad or address something that is already widely known; superficial question.

Notes/Modifications/Accommodations

This game should be played by students who already have some knowledge of how to develop research questions. The creativity and critical thinking necessary for this game could overwhelm students who have no understanding of research questions. If there is too much difference between what the students know and what they are expected to do, they may not engage in the game.

The number of cards within the deck can be changed depending on the amount of time allotted for the game. Two cards per person would be a good number for a short game. The number could increase from there, but it may be best to have an even number of cards for the number of people playing the game.

To keep the timing of the game under control, use a timer to limit how long each player can take to develop a research question. One minute would be a good limit. This would also be a good way to keep the game moving when a student is having trouble thinking up a research question but will not admit that they cannot do it.

Rather than have an individual debrief at the end of the game, it would be possible to have the students share what they learned with the entire class. It would be possible to perform an assessment at this time by checking that the points addressed in the rubric in table 9.2 are mentioned by the students. This also allows for any missing critical components to be addressed by the librarian.

The facts and ideas used for the cards can be easily customized for different classes. General information could be used for an introductory level class while discipline-specific information could be used for higher-level courses. It is also simple to interject some humor into the game with silly cards.

Below are a couple of lists of facts and ideas that can be used as starting points in printing off cards. For discipline-specific cards, it may be helpful to talk to the faculty member to provide content from the course. This is a way to help the students connect the work done in the lesson to the rest of their coursework.

General Deck of Facts and Ideas Cards—

- Men are more likely to be color blind than women.
- Hobbies help with stress.
- Carnivores eat meat.
- Vampires are stronger than humans.
- Music calms animals.
- Red and yellow make orange.
- Whales are mammals.
- Owls can rotate their heads up to 270 degrees.
- A megabyte is one million bytes.
- Shakespeare wrote *Macbeth*.
- Green is the best color for health.
- Writing something down helps you remember.
- Dystopian novels are set in the future.
- Diamonds are the hardest rocks.
- Monarch butterflies migrate during the winter.
- Water freezes at 32 degrees Fahrenheit.

Business Deck of Facts and Ideas Cards—

- NAICS codes are used to classify businesses.
- The GDP of the United States was about $17 trillion in 2013.
- FHA loans require a down payment.
- Small businesses are critical to the economy.
- Consumer confidence affects the economy.
- Segmenting your automated marketing is more effective.
- Fair-value accounting should always be used over hedge accounting.
- Accrual accounting records revenue and expenses when they are incurred.
- Marketing doctrine provides guidance in providing consistency.
- Customer loyalty programs increase brand awareness.
- Modigliani and Miller studied capital-structure theory in the 1950s.
- Just-in-Time stock control tries to keep costs to a minimum.
- Social security paid by a company is a deductible business expense.
- Zero-based budgeting requires all expenses to be justified each period.
- Blue-chip stocks are the leaders in their industry.
- An effective R&D department is critical for long-term growth.

Lesson Plan 3. Group Work
Lesson Plan Purpose

This lesson plan offers **reinforcement of the idea that research is composed of questions**. Students are expected to look at a preliminary research topic in more depth with the help of classmates.

Learning Objective

Students will consider the implications of various questions in order to develop a focused research question.

Audience

Students who have figured out a general topic for research, but have not yet narrowed the scope of their research. Class size from 2 to 200. Any level from undergraduates to graduate students.

Procedures

Time—30–35 minutes

Supplies—Method for the students to keep notes for themselves (computer or notebook).

Process—Students will need to be divided into groups of 3–4. Explain that during this time, the students will be working in groups and will be helping each other as they work to develop a research question. And since research involves looking for answers to questions, they will be helping each other only by asking questions. There will be no answers given today. Those are for later. Today is focused on generating questions.

Students will each have 5 minutes focused on their research. For the first 2 minutes, the individual students will share with their group their topic and everything they know about it. They can share what interests them about it and possible ideas they want to research. At the end of 2 minutes, time will be called. For the next 3 minutes, the rest of the group will provide questions to help focus and consider the topic. During these 3 minutes, only questions are to be asked. They can ask for more details, how the topic relates to something else, or any other question that would help focus the final research. While they are asking the questions, the student is recording each one. These questions are not going to be answered today, so the list is intended to provide guidance for continual research. After 3 minutes, time will be called again, and the process will be repeated with the next students until all students have shared their topics.

Once everyone has gone through the process, give the students 5 minutes to look through the questions asked by their group mates and pick the question or questions that they feel will be the most helpful as they continue their research. This question should be written down either on a sheet of paper to be handed in or in an e-mail message that can be sent to the librarian. Students should include with their questions an explanation of why this question will be helpful to them. If you feel the students are far enough along, you could have them include their preliminary research question with their response.

Assessment Opportunities

Formative Assessment—Formative assessment will take place as the librarian moves throughout the room during the group work and listens to the questions that are being asked by the students. The questions that will be asked should be varied and focused on the topics offered by their group mates.

Summative Assessment—Summative assessment will take place utilizing the question and analysis done by the student and handed in at the end of the group work. The rubric in table 9.3 offers some guidance on the scoring of the reply.

Table 9.3
Rubric for evaluating the research question and analysis

	Expert Learner	Intermediate Learner	Novice Learner
Understanding of topic	Notes how the question makes the researcher look more deeply into the topic by discovering what is unknown or controversial.	Notes that the question made them think about their topic in a new way.	Focuses on a question that reinforces their original understanding of topic.
Development of topic	Recognizes that there are a number of research questions and unknowns about the topic that they could develop further.	Notes that the topic may be more complex than they originally thought.	Focuses on one aspect of the topic exclusively.

Table 9.3
Rubric for evaluating the research question and analysis

	Expert Learner	Intermediate Learner	Novice Learner
Research question (if included)	Combines various concepts to examine a gap or conflict within the topic.	Combines various concepts within the field to look at a topic that may already be known.	Focuses upon one issue within the topic. This issue may be too broad or may address something that is already widely known; superficial question.

Notes/Modifications/Accommodations

If the students are having trouble thinking of questions to ask each other, you could have a list of prepared questions to get them started. Some possible questions include

- How long has this been an issue?
- Are there different positions on this topic? What proof do the different sides offer?
- Is there a specific group of people who are affected by this issue?
- How do you know what you do about the topic? Personal experience, books, classes, magazines?
- Are there other disciplines or majors that would also be interested in this?

By requiring the students to focus on asking each other questions, this lesson draws on the idea that research requires questions. Often, students focus solely on the answer. They have gotten used to the idea that the answer is the end product and is all that is required. This lesson shows that there are always more questions to be asked when conducting research.

Note

1. Association of College and Research Libraries, *Framework for Information Literacy for Higher Education* (Chicago: Association of College and Research Libraries, 2015), 7, http://www.ala.org/acrl/standards/ilframework.

Bibliography

Association of College and Research Libraries. *Framework for Information Literacy for Higher Education*. Chicago: Association of College and Research Libraries, 2015. http://www.ala.org/acrl/standards/ilframework.

CHAPTER 10

Framework Concept
Scholarship as Conversation

Communities of scholars, researchers, or professionals engage in sustained discourse with new insights and discoveries occurring over time as a result of varied perspectives and interpretations.[1]

Lesson Plan 1. Humor
Lesson Plan Purpose

This lesson plan offers students an **introduction to the concept of a seminal article**. Using an analogy as a prompt, students will list characteristics of a seminal article.

Learning Objective

Students will list characteristics of a seminal article in order to describe its importance to a particular field.

Audience

Undergraduates to lower-level graduate students. Class size from 5 to 200.

Procedures

Time—15 minutes

Supplies—Photo of Patient Zero (zombie) projected onto screen. White-board. Paper for minute paper.

Process—Project photo onto the screen.

LIBRARIAN'S SCRIPT: *This is Patient Zero and the start of the upcoming zombie apocalypse. Now in any zombie situation, there are those individuals who just lose their heads, start running around, and end up joining the mass of zombies. There are also those that just hole up and try to make it through. We, however, are going to be that group of people who are proactive and not only try to live, but also try to figure out what is happening so that we can defeat the zombies and save the world. Those people start out by thinking.*

So what we want to do is consider Patient Zero. What do we know about Patient Zero and his/her influence? Have the students list out characteristics and write them on the whiteboard. Some of the characteristics that they should be listing include Patient Zero is the first zombie; s/he infects everyone else; s/he is the start of a whole chain of events; once Patient Zero infects someone else, the impact gets multiplied as infections raise exponentially; and Patient Zero does not know the impact s/he will have.

After you have a list of characteristics, let the students know that thankfully it turns out that Patient Zero is not actually a zombie, so they do not have to worry about holding off a mass of dead, or undead, infected humans. But now that they have created such a nice list of characteristics on the board, you will turn the discussion to another topic—seminal articles. A seminal article is sometimes also referred to as a classic work, pivotal, or a landmark study. The seminal work is an article or book that is so original and groundbreaking that it influences everything that comes after it. So how can we connect the characteristics of Patient Zero with a seminal work?

The students should then go through the characteristics one at a time, with the librarian making comments as necessary. After the characteristics of a seminal work have been discussed, the students should be directed to answer the following question to be handed in after a minute: Why is it important to discover the seminal works on a particular topic?

Assessment Opportunities

Formative Assessment—The formative assessment takes place while the students are connecting the characteristics of a seminal work to the similar characteristics found in Patient Zero. By developing an initial list and then forming a definition of a seminal article, the students should be able to create connections between the two. This assessment will help guide the students to understand how a seminal work is a special work that influences others within a field for many years. The seminal work may start a whole new way to think about a topic.

Summative Assessment—The summative assessment will be done through an evaluation of the minute papers addressing the question "Why is it important to discover the seminal works within a particular topic?" The rubric in table 10.1 can be applied to the responses.

Table 10.1
Rubric for evaluating minute papers

	Expert Learner	**Intermediate Learner**	**Novice Learner**
Impact of seminal scholarship on ensuing conversation	Places the seminal work in perspective of how research on the topic will continue to change and evolve, noting that different ideas and individuals may hold differing views.	Notes that by finding the seminal work, you will be able to read other scholarship on the topic and have a better understanding of what is being discussed. This shows an understanding of the influence of the work and how it is best to follow a conversation throughout its entirety.	Notes that the seminal work has affected the conversation on the topic. May note that the author is "the" expert on the topic and thus his or her idea is correct.

Notes/Modifications/Accommodations

This lesson is meant as an introduction for students to the concept of the seminal article and how such a work will impact the conversation around the topic for many years. After this lesson, students may be taught how to find seminal works on their own, or they may be assigned to read a seminal work within their course by their instructor.

While the concept of Patient Zero can be found within a range of diseases, the topic of zombies is used for this lesson as it is a more lighthearted example. Zombies are also a well-known cultural icon, which means the concept should resonate with a number of the students. Depending on the students, zombie lore may also be something that has been frequently discussed.

In selecting an image to use for Patient Zero, it is probably best to avoid anything that is too gruesome as it may be disturbing for some students. A stock zombie image would work well. Another option would be to take the image of someone well known on campus, perhaps a willing course faculty member, and edit the image to look like a zombie by turning the face gray and adding some blood. This personal connection would add to the humor.

Lesson Plan 2. Game
Lesson Plan Purpose

This lesson plan offers **reinforcement of the concept of scholarship as an ongoing conversation**. Students will use citations found in articles to trace back the manner in which research creates a conversation that continues over many years.

Learning Objective

Students will analyze the citations of articles in order to discover how research continues over time.

Audience

Undergraduates through graduate students. Class size 5 to 200.

Procedures

Time—45–60 minutes

Supplies—Each student needs to have access to the Internet and library resources and worksheet (figure 10.1).

Process—

PURPOSE: To find the longest ongoing discussion of a research topic within three articles before time runs out.

BACKGROUND—LIBRARIAN'S SCRIPT: *You are all required to find articles for your classes. Usually the assignment is something like this: write a seven-page double-spaced paper in Times New Roman in twelve-point font with one-inch margins. You will need to cite five articles in APA style. So you set out to find those five articles. Hopefully before the night before it is due. Often you just grab those articles from a list of results without realizing that those results are often connected by more than just the keyword you typed in. These articles are part of an ongoing conversation on the topic, and as in any conversation, they are using what was said before to continue the discussion, come up with new ideas, and share information. They do that by citing other articles, just like you will do in that seven-page paper you are writing. It is important to know that these articles are not just things sitting out there in isolation, but are part of the ongoing conversation on the topic. Today you will take time to look in more depth at how individual articles connect to create a conversation that has been going on for years and will continue into the future. Your goal will be to find connecting articles that span the longest time frame in thirty minutes. Special points will go to the articles that have the most individuals taking part in the conversation (determined by the total number of articles cited in each article).*

GAME RULES:

1. Go to a periodical database. (Choice of database depends on those available to the students, the availability of full text, and the level and discipline of the students.)

2. Search any topic that interests you or that you think will have a long history.

3. Find an article published within the past year. This will be your first article; write down the citation on the worksheet.

4. Go to the works cited or references at the end of the article. Count the number of references. Put that number on the worksheet. Find the oldest article.

5. Write down the citation of the oldest article on the worksheet. This is your second article. Find this article. (If at any point you cannot get full text access to the oldest article, choose another article to find.)

6. Go to the works cited or references at the end of the second article. Count the number of references. Put that number on the worksheet. Find the oldest article.

7. Write down the citation of the oldest article on the worksheet. This is the third and final article that you must find. Find the full text of this article.

8. Go to the works cited or references at the end of the article. Count the number of references. Add that number to the worksheet. Find the oldest article.

9. Write down the citation of the oldest article on the worksheet. Subtract the year of that article from the year of the first article. This is the length of the conversation.

10. Add up the number of citations from the three articles and enter that number.

11. When the time is up, everyone shares the length of their conversation. Ties will be broken by the number of articles cited.

12. When the winner has been declared, answer the final questions on the worksheet.

Article 1:	Citation
	Number of References
Article 2:	Citation
	Number of References
Article 3:	Citation
	Number of References
Oldest Article:	Citation
Length of conversation:	
Total number of cited articles:	

Questions:
1. Look at the titles of the articles you listed. Was there a shift in focus or in the way they approached the topic? How might scholarship on a topic change over time?
2. Did you notice any of the same names or articles appearing in the citations of the different articles? What does it tell you about an author or a specific article if it is cited in multiple other articles?

FIGURE 10.1

Worksheet

Assessment Opportunities

Formative Assessment—The formative assessment will take place while the students are answering the final questions on the worksheet. During this time, it is possible to see if the students are having trouble answering the questions and if they are asking for assistance.

Summative Assessment—The summative assessment will analyze the answers to the final questions on the worksheet. The rubric in table 10.2 can be applied to the questions.

Table 10.2 Rubric for evaluation of questions on worksheet			
	Expert Learner	**Intermediate Learner**	**Novice Learner**
Evolution of scholarship conversation	Discusses the fact that the research on a topic continues to evolve and shift throughout the years as different individuals take part in the discussions, and that various perspectives may become more or less prevalent. Recognizes that there may not be one "right" answer within the research. May also note that events outside of the field may affect the research.	Discusses how the conversation within the field may change as new individuals study the topic.	Notes a basic understanding that new ideas or discoveries could be made that would add to the research discussion. May show a dualistic nature of information by noting that the old ideas were wrong and the new ideas are correct.

Table 10.2
Rubric for evaluation of questions on worksheet

	Expert Learner	Intermediate Learner	Novice Learner
Influence of different voices within the conversation	Discusses how the heavy presence of a single author signifies an influence on the topic that may either indicate the importance of the author or mean the author's ideas are overwhelming the discussion, which stifles other ideas.	In addition to noting that a frequently cited author would be considered an expert in a topic, also notes that that author will have influence on how the discussion surrounding the topic gets structured.	Notes that an author who is cited frequently is an expert in the topic.

Notes/Modifications/Accommodations

This game works better if students have some familiarity with using databases and searching for a known item. Even with familiarity, it may be beneficial to model the process of finding articles and using the citations to find additional articles as an example to start the game. This may also provide the students with a starting goal, as they try to find a chain of articles that are older than the one used as an example.

While this lesson asks each student to conduct a search individually in order to provide the most hands-on experience, it would be possible to organize the students into groups. This shift would be useful in cases where there is limited computer access or in very large classes. Depending on the time constraints of the class, it is possible to decrease or increase the number of articles the students are expected to find.

An added benefit of this lesson is that it requires the students to use several additional skills. First, they must work within a database in order to find articles, limit results, and get access to the full text. Second, it has them look at the citations of articles in order to find related resources. This is a skill that is often discussed and encouraged, but one that lower-level students may not fully utilize. At a more basic level, looking at the citations also requires students to know how to read a citation in order to determine the date and publication title. Finally, this lesson asks them to find articles from known citations. This is another skill that students may not fully utilize, preferring to just use the full text of articles they retrieve from a search.

Lesson Plan 3. Group Work
Lesson Plan Purpose

This lesson plan provides an **introduction to the idea of scholarship as a conversation**. Students will see how they are a part of the conversation and how the conversation can occur through a range of media.

Learning Objective

Students will list a range of venues for information in order to develop a framework on how different information venues interconnect.

Audience

Lower- to mid-level undergraduates. Class size 6 to 25.

Procedures

Time—20–30 minutes

Supplies—A ball of yarn. Space to form a circle. Paper for group concept map.

Process—Ask the students to stand up and form a circle. Take a place in the circle with the ball of yarn. Introduce yourself to a student beside you. Ask the student's name, and have them share their passion, the thing that they would be doing if they were not in class. Tell them that they have just come up with a great, amazing idea related to their passion, and the ball of yarn represents that idea. So now that they have this great idea, they want to share it with everyone. Ask them how they share ideas with others; when they come up with something, how do they let others know? After they have noted how they share information, have them hold onto the end of the yarn and throw the ball to someone else. The ball and yarn represent their idea going out into the world. Ask the student who now has the ball what options they have at this point. (It can either stop there or that individual can pass on the idea as well.) Have the student share how they spread information. They hold onto the yarn and throw it to another student. This process continues as each student notes how they would share the information. As they hold onto the yarn, a web will be formed of overlapping yarn. Try to encourage students to be specific in how they share the information, so not just "social media" but a specific platform. Also, try to encourage different methods of how the information is shared, but do not be too strict if they cannot think of an original idea.

Once everyone has shared and is holding a part of the web, it is time to begin the discussion. Start by asking the students why they just made this web. Their responses are a great way to see their understanding on the topic. Now tell the students that someone outside of the web has started doing research and has jumped into the conversation web. Ask the students, what is this person learning as he or she moves across the web? Are the different types of venues (Facebook post, YouTube video, published article) providing different types of information? How does the venue affect what he or she thinks about the information?

After the interconnections of the conversation are discussed, go on by asking what happens if parts of this informational web leave? If people change their mind on supporting the idea or come up with a different idea? Then have several of the individuals drop the yarn. The web will weaken and the great idea is not as strong. Note that ideas that were once accepted can change with new evidence, so it is always important when trying to take part in a conversation on a topic to stay involved in order to see how it is evolving.

After the discussion, have the final students drop their yarn. At this time, tell the students that they will now have the chance to work together to create a concept map that incorporates the ideas that they just discussed. Divide the students into groups of 4. Each group will be given a sheet of paper on which to create their concept map. Share some examples of generic concept maps to get the students started.

CONCEPT MAP SHEET DIRECTIONS: Within your group you will create a concept map. A concept map takes different ideas and lays them out in an organized fashion. Items are grouped and connected with lines noting their relationship. The concept map you create will look at the conversation that occurs around a topic. When developing ideas and keywords to add to your concept map, consider things such as how the information is shared, who provides the information, who uses the information, and how these items overlap and connect.

Assessment Opportunities

Formative Assessment—The formative assessment takes place during the discussion around the web. Students should be able to talk about how the various types of people providing the piece of information affects the type and usefulness of that information in different contexts.

Summative Assessment—The summative assessment will look at the concept map created by the groups. The rubric in table 10.3 can be used to analyze the final project.

Table 10.3 Rubric for evaluating concept maps			
	Expert Learner	**Intermediate Learner**	**Novice Learner**
Venues within conversation	Notes how the type of information presented in different venues affects who is putting information out within that venue and how they present and discuss the topic within the venue.	Shows an understanding that different venues provide outputs for different individuals to share information.	Does not differentiate between the authors and consumers of information in different venues.

Notes/Modifications/Accommodations

Students provide a range of methods used to share information. They will often propose various types of media including written, oral, visual, and multimedia. The lesson itself is meant to provide a rapid accumulation of a number of ideas. For those classes that already have some knowledge on information venues, it would be possible to have the students give a little more detail about the type of information they would provide, for example, "I would write a blog that would give an overview for people with no knowledge on the topic," or "I would create a video for YouTube that explains the process in more depth so people could get additional information."

The concept map is created through group effort as a way for the students to share more of their ideas with a smaller audience. The group allows them to generate more ideas than they would on their own as well as to form connections between ideas that they may not have developed by themselves.

This lesson can be used as an introduction to a more in-depth look at the different types of resources available to students, for example, the differences between popular and scholarly works. For upper-level students, it could be used as the starting point to look at the various outlets they could use to start getting their work published and shared in their field.

Note

1. Association of College and Research Libraries, *Framework for Information Literacy for Higher Education* (Chicago: Association of College and Research Libraries, 2015), 8, http://www.ala.org/acrl/standards/ilframework.

Bibliography

Association of College and Research Libraries. *Framework for Information Literacy for Higher Education*. Chicago: Association of College and Research Libraries, 2015. http://www.ala.org/acrl/standards/ilframework.

CHAPTER 11

Framework Concept
Searching as Strategic Exploration

Searching for information is often nonlinear and iterative, requiring the evaluation of a range of information sources and the mental flexibility to pursue alternate avenues as new understanding develops.[1]

Lesson Plan 1. Humor
Lesson Plan Purpose

This lesson plan offers an **introduction to the concept of subject headings**. Students will consider word choice and how these decisions change based on audience and circumstance.

Learning Objective

Students will recognize the difference between subject headings and keywords in order to use them effectively when conducting a search.

Audience

Lower-level students. Class size from 1 to 250.

Procedures

Time—10 minutes

Supplies—For Example One, samples of texting acronym failures. For Example Two, whiteboard.

Example One—

Start by sharing a miscommunication between two people because one of them is using an acronym that the other does not understand. This is the humor that will motivate them to focus on the content. (Text messaging errors can be found online to be used as examples.)

LIBRARIAN'S SCRIPT: *This is what can happen when people try to communicate, but one of them uses words that are not understood by both. It is best to match up the language used with the individual you are speaking to. Think about the last party you attended. Who was there? What did you do? Tell me about it.* Have a student share a 10-second short story. *Now, how would you tell your grandmother about it? Now how would you tell a friend who was not there? You see, there are different ways to describe the same event.*

In a similar way, there are different ways to search for sources. The most common way that you search is by using keywords. Everyone can think of their own keywords. They are found throughout the source and will often appear in a title or summary. Then there are things called subject headings. These are terms that have been taken from a previously developed list and applied to the source. They provide a controlled vocabulary on what the source is about, even if the words themselves are not in the article. Subject headings are helpful in that someone has connected a source with a specific word or phrase. It is a better way to ensure that the source pertains to a topic rather than just hoping a keyword will bring back an accurate result. Also, think of the words that have more than one meaning. A keyword will bring back just sources that contain that word. A subject search will bring back sources on the topic you are looking for.

Example Two—

LIBRARIAN'S SCRIPT: *You are here because you are about to start a new research paper. And the first thing you want to do in this process is find an-*

other class that does not make you do research. (Insert rimshot.) *Actually, what you need to do is pick a topic. I have already picked a topic, so now you are all going to help me start my research process. What I need from you now is to help think of keywords for my search. For my research, I will be looking up prisons. This choice has nothing to do with the fact that Nicolas Cage is in The Rock. It does, however, have something to do with the fact that Sean Connery is in The Rock and that Scottish accents are one of the two best accents in the world. So back to my keywords. One important thing when developing keywords is to think of possible synonyms or other words that could be used. So what are other terms I could use besides prison?*

List the words provided by the students on the whiteboard. If they are having trouble, start the list with some more obscure terms. Lists of slang terms can be found before the class.

So, it turns out that there are a lot more words for prison that I had thought. Now I really do not want to do a search for each of these keywords. I could pick out ones that I thought would be the most popular, but an even better way would be if there was a word that everyone agreed to use when talking about sources on this topic. And I am here to tell you that there is an agreed-upon word. In the library, these words are called subject headings. These are terms that have been taken from a previously developed list and applied to the source. They provide a controlled vocabulary on what the source is about, even if the words themselves are not in the source. They are a very useful thing to know about when you are conducting research, because even if the authors are using different terms, someone has applied a subject heading so that you can find all the sources on your topic.

Assessment Opportunities

Formative Assessment—As this lesson focuses on the instruction librarian's short lecture, formative assessment will be conducted mainly through informal methods such as looking for comprehension or confusion on the faces of the students. It would also be possible after the lesson to ask if there are any questions or to have someone define keywords and subject headings. Having a student offer a definition is often a great way to not only find out if they understand the topic, but also allow for another reiteration of the content in case others did not understand.

Summative Assessment—A true assessment of whether students have internalized this concept would be to observe whether they use subject headings as appropriate when conducting a search. This level of detail is not available within this short lecture lesson.

One method to see if students have understood this concept would be to have them fill out a one-minute paper at the end of the session in which they provide something they learned. This would give an indication of whether they understood the lesson and what they may have learned from it.

Another possible assessment on whether students have understood the difference between keywords and subject headings would be a question included in some sort of test. Some institutions have their students complete a short quiz after completing information literacy instruction. A question could be included that asks them to differentiate between a keyword and subject heading.

Notes/Modifications/Accommodations

This lesson is really a short introduction to the idea of subject headings. It would be possible to go into more depth on how subject headings are created, but this was designed to be a way to let students know that there are different ways to search. In some fields, such as for medical students, controlled vocabulary can take on a greater importance. To expand this lesson, after going through one of the examples, it would be possible to demonstrate how to use and where to find the subject headings in different databases.

One method to set the tone for the class and provide content to discuss later would be to have one or a series of texting acronym failures being projected on a screen as the students are entering the class. This way they see the miscommunication, experience humor, and are prepared for the later discussion.

It may be nice to have a range of acronym failures to present, as this gives the students several opportunities to experience the humor. If they do not understand one of the texts or do not find it funny, they may understand and find another humorous. In looking for humorous text acronyms, a search for text fails or text acronym fails will produce a number of results to choose from.

One note for texting acronyms: Often the miscommunication stems from either sexual context or inappropriate language. These types of texts may not be appropriate for your classroom. It is up to you to select examples that you feel are appropriate.

When choosing a sample topic to look up in the second example, it is best to use one with a number of synonyms. The humorous aside related to the movie *The Rock* is an example of a personal connection that promotes relatability between the librarian and students. Any number of examples could be used as relevant to the individual librarian.

Lesson Plan 2. Game

Lesson Plan Purpose

This lesson plan offers an introduction to the **variety of sources available when answering a question**. Students use experience and creativity to brainstorm sources before considering which are the most appropriate.

Learning Objective

Students will generate an extensive list of possible sources for an information need in order to explore various options before determining the most appropriate sources.

Audience

Varied. Versions of this game can be used with any group of students from freshmen up to graduate students. Class size from 2 to 50. Difficulty can be added by changing the initial information need to be researched.

Procedures

Time—15–20 minutes

Supplies—Computer access for each student or paper and pencil. Whiteboard. Clock or timer.

Process: Game Rules—

PURPOSE: Earn points by coming up with a unique source in order to answer a research question. The individual with the most points at the end is the winner.

GAME PLAY—INTRODUCTION—LIBRARIAN'S SCRIPT: *Thanks for playing "Sources, Sources, Everywhere, but Which One Should I Pick?" the game that tests your creativity and knowledge of all the different places you can go to find information. The rules are simple, but the challenge is hard as we locate the best resources. To start off the game, I will provide you with an information need. You will then have three minutes to brainstorm all of the possible sources that could help you answer the question. Record your answers on paper or in a file that you can send to me.*

1. Give the students a question for which they can brainstorm possible sources.

2. After time has been called, have one student state the first source on their list. Librarian records source on the whiteboard.

3. Ask if anyone else has also listed that source. Everyone who has that source marks it with an *X*, removing it from their total number of sources.

4. If anyone does not feel that the source helps answer the information need, they can declare a challenge. After being challenged, the student with the source on their list must give a reason why the source would be useful. The librarian offers the final say on whether the source will be included.

5. The next student states their first unmarked source. Librarian records the source on the whiteboard. Students call out if they have the same source. Challenges are made as necessary.

6. This process continues with a new student naming their source until all of the sources brainstormed have been called.

7. After all the sources have been listed, the students count up their sources that do not have an *X*. The one with the most unique sources wins.

CONCLUSION/NEXT STEP: After declaring a winner, discuss how this game shows the great variety of sources that are available in which students can find information. This moves the conversation to a discussion of how to utilize the best sources for different information needs. From the list on the board, have the students choose the most appropriate sources. This allows for an understanding that not all sources are equal, and the appropriateness of a source depends on the initial information need.

EXAMPLE: The information need is "When does the grocery store close tonight?" Students brainstorm for 3 minutes. Abe shares his first source, "I'd call the store." The librarian writes *call the store* on the board. Several students yell that they have it on their list. They each mark it with an *X*. Ben shares his next source, "I'd look at a store flyer." The librarian writes *store flyer* on the board. No one else has store flyer on their list, so Ben gets one point. Cate shares her next source, "I'd ask my roommate Daniel." The librarian writes *Daniel* on the board. No one else has Daniel on their list. Someone calls out challenge. Cate says that Daniel works at the grocery store. The librarian judges that this experience makes Daniel a good source for the information, so Cate gets one point.

Assessment Opportunities

Formative Assessment—The challenges issued during the game can be a great way to determine students' understanding of the purpose and content of various sources. The explanation of the usefulness of a source may demonstrate an understanding of authority, bias, reliability, or a range of other criteria.

Summative Assessment—Collect the source lists brainstormed by the students. These can either be collected after the game if on paper or e-mailed to the librarian. The rubric in table 11.1 can be used in a quantitative and qualitative review of the sources listed by the student. This rubric can be modified as applicable based on the information need presented by the librarian.

Table 11.1
Rubric for evaluating source lists

	Expert Learner	**Intermediate Learner**	**Novice Learner**
Number of sources	5+	3–5	1–2
Types of sources	Provides a broad range of sources from the general Internet, print publications, and experts.	Lists primarily one type of source with some variety.	Lists only one type of source, e.g., all websites.
Specificity of sources	Notes appropriate library databases or websites or professionals.	Notes specific type of website, e.g., .org website or generic library databases.	Lists broad categories, e.g., Google, the library.

Notes/Modifications/Accommodations

The information need developed by the librarian at the beginning of the game allows for endless variety. It allows the game to be played across all levels of instruction, for example, for entry-level students "What fat is good for you?" and for graduate students "How has the understanding of the impact of unsaturated fats developed?" This game is also a great way to introduce students to various resources when they have a specific assignment that requires them to do research.

This game can easily be played by groups rather than individuals. The groups may need to keep their best sources quiet so that they are not taken by another group. One method to keep their ideas secret would be to use a shared online space such as Google Docs where they can list their sources.

For a more in-depth game, after each source, have the students write down one sentence reflecting the reason they chose that source. This will delve deeper into their understanding of the benefits and characteristics of various sources and allow for a more nuanced assessment. It would also be possible to have the students list sources for two questions. These questions should be varied to show that sometimes a simple web search will provide an answer, while other times it is necessary to find more focused resources.

If you are finding too many students simply note Google as their only response, take time to note that Google is not a source in itself. Google is a way to find sources. The sources are the results that are returned after a Google search.

This lesson also encourages students to think creatively about possible information sources. Inform the students that there is no wrong answer as long as they have a reason for how the source would help answer the question. The more creative the students are in coming up with a range of sources, the more likely they are to win the game.

Lesson Plan 3. Group Work
Lesson Plan Purpose

This lesson plan offers a reinforcement of **how to search within a specific library database**. Students will need to explore various features of the database in order to find a resource. They will then explain their search process and why they chose their resource.

Learning Objective

Students will demonstrate an understanding of how to search for information utilizing a database in order to find an appropriate source.

Audience

Lower level classes. Classes of 24 or fewer.

Procedures

Time—20 minutes plus 5 minutes for each group to present

Supplies—Internet access for the students. Projector and screen for group presentations. Research question(s).

Process—Break up the class into groups. Four students per group works well. No more than 6 students per group. After the students are in their groups, provide an introduction and explanation of the activity.

INTRODUCTION—LIBRARIAN'S SCRIPT: *So often when you are required to do research, you think only about the final source that you use. Today we are not only going to think about that source, but we are also going to focus on the journey to get to that source. Let's say you want to get to the mall because your mother told you it was the best place to buy her a present. So you have an end goal in mind, but you have never been to the mall before because you do all your shopping on Amazon. So you just hop in the car and start driving around figuring that sooner or later you will end up finding the mall. And amazingly you do get there and buy her present. However, you didn't pay any attention to how you got there. Now, your dad wants you to pick him up something from the mall. You now have to again just randomly wander around in your car until you find the mall. A more successful plan would have included paying attention to how you got to the mall and figuring out shortcuts and tricks to make the trip easier.*

This is similar to finding sources for research papers or projects. Your professor is asking you to find this specific thing, but you have never used anything like it. So you go out and poke around until you find a source that you can use. You are happy, you write the paper, and all is good. That is, until your next professor asks you to find a source, and you do not remember how you found the first one. If you just blindly search until something comes up, you will be wasting your time. A better approach is to pay attention to how you searched. Were there specific keywords or search techniques that you used? Could you use limiters or other ways to refine your search? These details are all a part of the journey to the final source. By learning how to use these details you will have a much smoother trip. Today we are going to share with each other our journeys in finding sources.

You have been divided up into groups. Each group will be given a re-search question. You will have fifteen minutes to use the database (the choice of database depends on the library's subscription and needs of the students, depending on the research they will be required to do for the class) *to find a source that helps answer the question.*

One person in the group will need to be the recorder. The recorder will be the one making the "map" of the research journey. It is the recorder's job to keep track of things such as which keywords you used to search, how many results you got back, if you changed keywords, if you used a limiter in the da-tabase, if you went to the second page of results, and so on. This map is very important, as it is what you will be presenting to your classmates. For your presentation you will use the projector to show each step and explain your thoughts as you went through the journey. You will then show us the source that you chose and very briefly tell why you chose it.

The journey itself will be up to you. You can work together to come up with keywords and do one search, or you can try different searches to find your final source. No matter how you do it, just remember to record the steps you took and the reasons why you took them.

1. Students break into groups. The librarian should circulate to answer questions as they arise.

2. Students start their presentations, providing the steps in their search process and thought process. As necessary, the librarian should ask questions, prompting them to provide more detail on why they did certain things.

Assessment Opportunities

Formative Assessment—The fifteen minutes while the students are pre-paring their presentation will provide the opportunity to conduct some formative assessment. This can occur in two ways. First, as the students talk to each other, it will be possible to hear what they understand about the process and what they are having trouble with. At times, students illus-trate a deeper understanding talking to each other than they will share in a presentation. Second, you will be able to determine their understanding based on the questions they ask. If a couple of groups have similar ques-tions, it may be best to relay the answer to the entire class as a topic that needs to be clarified.

Summative Assessment—The presentation on the research process and source chosen to answer the research question provide the opportunity to gain an understanding of the thought process behind the searching done by students. This allows for a more complete understanding of their knowledge than can be gleaned from looking at a list of citations. The rubric in table 11.2 can be completed as the students are giving their presentations.

Table 11.2
Rubric for assessing student presentations

	Expert Learner	**Intermediate Learner**	**Novice Learner**
Able to refine search strategies based on results	Clearly states why choices were made in relation to keyword choice and search refinements in order to obtain a relevant source.	Refined search but does not offer reasons for how the refined search would result in better sources.	Did no refinement of the search. Simply chose source from first results.
Keyword choice	Considers and uses a range of keywords such as synonyms and jargon.	Combines keywords to focus search.	Relies on one basic keyword.
Utilization of database	Uses advanced search features, limiters, and other search refinement features.	Uses basic search with a limited use of search refinement features.	Only uses basic search feature.
Source selection	Clearly states why source was selected using several applicable evaluative criteria.	Provides limited explanation of evaluative criteria or may use evaluative criteria that are not applicable to the research need.	Explanation of source selection contains no reference to evaluative criteria.

Notes/Modifications/Accommodations

This lesson can be easily used to expose students to any number of periodical databases, the library catalog, websites, or search engines. The students get a hands-on opportunity to use the resources to find useful sources as well as the chance to learn different tricks or search techniques from each other.

When providing research questions to the class, each group could have a different question, or the entire class could look up the same question. It may be informative to the students to see how others approached the same question and how they were able to manipulate the results.

For the students to be able to successfully choose a source, it may be best for them to have already discussed evaluation criteria. Also, if the professor is requiring them to use a certain type of source, such as peer-reviewed sources, this is a great opportunity for them to learn how to find and identify such a source.

Note

1. Association of College and Research Libraries, *Framework for Information Literacy for Higher Education* (Chicago: Association of College and Research Libraries, 2015), 9, http://www.ala.org/acrl/standards/ilframework.

Bibliography

Association of College and Research Libraries. *Framework for Information Literacy for Higher Education.* Chicago: Association of College and Research Libraries, 2015. http://www.ala.org/acrl/standards/ilframework.

Conclusion

The lesson plans detailed within this book are not meant to provide a complete curriculum for offering information literacy instruction. Rather, they provide parts of instruction that can be mixed and matched as necessary within an individual program. It is critical to note that all colleges and universities and courses and class sections are different, and as such, they require an individualized approach. There is no one correct way to present and instruct students. While it is possible to implement the lesson plans as presented in part II of the book as they are written, readers are also encouraged to use aspects of the lessons as they see fit and as applicable to their situation and needs.

Even if the lesson plans are not implemented in any form, I hope that they will at least provide some inspiration to utilize various instructional techniques that incorporate fun within the library classroom. Fun can be approached in a myriad of ways, and when used to motivate students rather than entertain, it can be a powerful tool to aid in the understanding of rigorous content. When fun is able to stimulate students to engage with the content of the threshold concepts, the likelihood of those students comprehending and applying these concepts in the future is increased.

When used consciously and purposefully, fun provides a range of benefits in the classroom. First, fun is a way to motivate students to pay attention. With an increasing number of distractions entering the classroom in the form of laptops, tablets, and smartphones, it is critical that we find ways to keep students present. If the students are not paying attention, there is no way they will be able to learn. Fun, whether through humor, games, or group work, pulls the students from a passive state and draws their attention to the content.

Second, fun has the ability to motivate students and keep them focused on the material. If students are enjoying themselves, they will continue to work through problems. The ability of fun to connect with the factors that promote intrinsic motivation results in students who will work longer on a problem and try to overcome more difficulties that may arise within that work. This ability of fun to promote extended engagement with the content allows for more rigorous content to be covered.

Connecting the content with fun also results in a positive relationship for future encounters. This type of behavioral conditioning stems from prior experiences. If something was positive in the past, someone is more likely to continue than if it was negative. This positive relationship can also result in better recall of the material. The experience of fun provides a prompt that links the content in a way that it is more easily remembered.

Finally, fun provides benefits for the instructor beyond the instructional aids for students. When implementing instructional techniques that involve fun in the classroom, the instructor should also participate in the fun. These instructional techniques are often new for instructors, and this novelty staves off some monotony and burnout that may occur. The use of fun also results in a different experience every class. Compared to a lecture or a canned demonstration, there is no way to predict for sure what will happen when implementing some of these lesson plans. While this unknown factor may worry some individuals, it does provide energy in the classroom. As librarians, we feel a passion and interest for our discipline. By utilizing fun, we are able to share this delight with students and help them appreciate what information literacy is and how it can be a part of their lives.

Library instruction is always interesting, but with the new *Framework for Information Literacy for Higher Education*, we are at a time of change and possibility in exploring new outcomes and techniques. The threshold concepts listed in the *Framework* provide a structure that allows us to consider information literacy as an intellectual construct in addition to manual skills. To fully master these concepts, it is critical to have multiple exposures to and experiences with them. The lesson plans provided allow students the opportunity to engage in aspects of the six threshold concepts with fun used as a motivational means to encourage that engagement. The eighteen plans cover various aspects of the threshold concepts geared toward a range of students and levels of understanding. The instructional techniques that utilize fun in this book allow librarians to move students from Novice to Expert status within the threshold concepts of the *Framework for Information Literacy for Higher Education*. Just as we encourage students to always learn, so too should we as librarians push ourselves to utilize new instructional approaches as we teach.